Given to Sr Teresa Margaret
April 18, 1964

JOY IN THE SPIRITUAL LIFE

Joy in the Spiritual Life

By

Bernard J. Kelly, C.S.Sp., D.D., D.Litt.

THE NEWMAN PRESS
WESTMINSTER · MARYLAND

248
KcJ

First published 1961

Permissu Superiorum

© *Copyright by* CLONMORE & REYNOLDS LTD.

MADE AND PRINTED IN THE REPUBLIC OF IRELAND BY
SEALY BRYERS & WALKER LTD. FOR CLONMORE &
REYNOLDS LTD. NIHIL OBSTAT: IOANNES O'DONOGHUE
CENSOR DEPUT. IMPRIMI POTEST: ✠ IOANNES
CAROLUS, ARCHIEPISCOPUS DUBLINEN. HIBERNIÆ
PRIMAS. DIE 31 AUG., 1960.

CONTENTS

Immaculata Conceptio tua Dei Genitrix Virgo,
Gaudium annuntiavit universo mundo.
(Versicle for Feast of the Immaculate Conception)

Your Immaculate Conception, Virgin Mother of God,
Brought tidings of joy to the whole world.

AUTHOR'S PREFACE

Joy is an important element in the christian life. In the pages which follow I endeavour to show just how important it is. The treatment of the subject is popular rather than strictly theological, but every effort has been made to avoid vagueness and looseness of expression.

Occasionally the reader may be tempted to wonder what can be the practical value of particular chapters or sections in helping him to find more joy in his life. Though dealing with joy they may strike him as somewhat speculative and remote from actual living. I should like to anticipate his difficulty by reminding him of the genuine practical assistance we derive from an enlightened mind. One of the things aimed at in the more theoretical parts of the book is to build up a mind or outlook in which there will be a due appreciation of the place of joy in our approach to God through Jesus. Granted such a mind we shall certainly, by God's grace, find joy. Without it there is serious danger of making life joyless for no better reason than that joy is suspect or ignored.

A final point I should like to make is that joy is not found mainly through reading but through living. And living is a matter of giving: he who loses his life by spending it for God and souls finds it. It would be a serious error to twist the spiritual life into a pursuit of joy. Most assuredly there is joy to be found in it. But it is found by seeking God and souls, not by being itself sought. And having found it the soul is impelled to return with all the greater ardour to a never-wearying giving of self. May God grant that these few pages be of assistance to souls in their efforts to throw themselves without reserve into the glorious undertaking of an unselfish life.

Holy Ghost Missionary College,
Kimmage, Dublin.
Feast of the Immaculate Conception, December 8th, 1960.

1

IN QUEST OF JOY

THE African sun was, as usual, merciless. Even in the car, with the windows open and a speed-made artificial breeze blowing hard through, it was impossible to escape fully from the fierce heat. And there they stood at the roadside thumbing a lift, a young man and a younger woman, their knapsacks pressing hard on their shoulders, and the dust of I knew not how many scorching miles on their feet. I stopped and took them in. I forgot what language they spoke. They were from some part of Europe and had decided to spend their honeymoon hiking across Africa. I was able to shorten their journey by about fifty miles. After that they would walk on till they met the next motorist.

We did not talk much for they were tired. I gathered that they slept wherever they could, ate what they could get, risked whatever dangers their way held. I gathered also that they were enjoying themselves, even though they were worn-out, travel-stained and occasionally hungry. They were doing something they wanted to do and putting up with the inevitable inconveniences. Totted up, it amounted to happiness.

More and more people seek happiness in strange ways. But there is nothing strange in seeking happiness. We all do that. No man can get on without happiness. One finds it in one way of life and another in another. One finds more and another less. One finds duty a source of happiness and another tries to squeeze a little of it in between rounds of

9

irksome duties. But no one is content to be wholly without it. God made man for happiness and no man escapes the thirst for it which God has implanted in him. Men differ only in how they quench it. Some misunderstand its insatiability and try feverishly to quench it at the wrong springs. The thirst is good: the drink they take is poison.

Christianity is God's way to man's happiness. The christian life is essentially a joyous one. Without joy christianity cannot be fully understood: "These things have I spoken to you that my joy may be in you, and your joy may be filled".[1] Christmas is a joyous feast. Easter and Ascension Day are more than joyous: they are triumphant. How is it, then, that joy often counts for so little in the life of the priest, religious and layman?

Two answers suggest themselves. One, that many do not understand the importance of joy. The other, that many miss the full scope of christianity.

To some it sounds odd—improper even—to speak of the importance of joy. The importance of duty they will admit, the importance of justice and charity and patience, the importance of self-denial—most certainly do they see the importance of patience and self-denial. But joy, they believe, is optional in God's designs: something to be detached from if it is given, and not to be sought if it is withheld.

The truth is that joy is a necessity. It is a necessity first of all in that christianity is going to make you joyous unless you hinder it. Joy is a consequence of doing a thing you want to do. The more and the deeper you want to do it the more joy it brings. If you are a christian and want to be a christian you are going to be joyous with every breath of your christian life whether you advert to the fact or no. Every right thing you do and want to do is going to be the occasion of joy. Of course a christian remains a fallen man, and there are things which he does and wants to do as a christian but which do not appeal at all to the old Adam in him. Then there will be

[1] Jo. 15, 11.

a conflict within him, joy striving with sorrow, joy in virtue striving with the sad baulked hankering after sin. Or it may be that the sorrow springs from physical pain. But the battle-field where the soul strives to conquer life is broad enough and to spare for both sorrow and joy. Sorrow of one kind may be there with joy of another; the joy of being a christian may be pressed hard by pain, but it need not be put to flight. Or, to change the image, your joy may not always be un-clouded, but it will never cease to be while God's grace is still in your soul. Joy and the christian life are so wed that one cannot be without the other.

Joy is necessary in another sense also. The less joy a person finds in christianity the less of himself he will put into being a christian. The Lord loves a cheerful giver not only because of the cheerfulness with which he gives but also because his cheerfulness makes him give more and more gladly. A certain type of literature has idealized the man who lives for honour and duty only and in whose life there is no place for the joys and sorrows which spring from friendship given and refused, praise and blame, appreciation and ingratitude. Joy and sorrow cannot be so dismissed as if of no account. To be sure, it is necessary to order one's attitude to them: but to ignore them would be to cultivate a psychology of make-believe, to mistake a subtle form of escapism for a sublime form of high devotion. The right kind of joy releases—one might almost say creates—energy. Cold insensibility is sub-human rather than angelic. It can be achieved only by weakening or damping down one's life-energy. Whatever the efficiency of the joyless man in certain restricted fields, he is at a disadvantage in the essential business of living. One can conceive of a joyless industrial magnate but not of a joyless saint.

*   *   *   *

To what extent is it true to say that to miss the import-ance of joy is to miss the full meaning of christianity?

Christianity is in itself a completely simple thing, like the life of God in which it is a sharing. Being a sharing in God's

life, it is not ultimately the result of adding a number of
parts together, and for that reason its full meaning is not
arrived at by adding idea to idea. But being sublime as well
as simple, we can express it in terms adapted to our capacity
only through a number of concepts. It is somewhat like a
mathematical problem which can be all summed up in one
glance by a good mathematician but which ordinary mortals
can grasp only when it is spread over page after page of
symbols. Now, the great saints have a feel, a kind of instinctive appreciation, for the inner meaning of christianity. They
seize it in its simplicity and this safeguards them against the
danger of knowing it only in part and thinking they have
grasped the whole. To less saintly men christianity appears
a complex way of life with aspect balancing aspect and no
one thing running unchanged through its complexity. And
with so many aspects and so much complexity, something
will surely be overlooked. Hence the striking lacunae found
in the christian mind of so many catholics—good people
who lack appreciation of self-denial, or the sacraments, or
Our Lady, or the missions. They are christian, but not fully:
they have the mind of Christ, but not His whole mind. I am
not thinking now of the objective implications of the
formulae which they accept on the Church's authority. In
every act of faith they accept the whole of christianity by
accepting all that the Church teaches. I am considering the
subjective side of the question, what they hold in detail and
explicitly as opposed to globally and implicitly. For it is
what they hold in detail and explicitly that most of all they
work into daily life. Does not the Imitation remind us of
how possible this error is when it warns against discoursing
deeply of the Trinity while lacking humility, which is an
offence against the Trinity? It follows that one can be quite
a good christian, up to a point, and still miss the fact that
joy is an element in christianity: just as one could miss or
be hazy about the importance of so many other things. In
fact, something is always being missed, and to be sure of
coming eventually to a worthy understanding of the faith

one must be utterly convinced from the beginning that there is always more, far more, in it than can be seen at any particular moment. Joy is most definitely in it. Just glance through the Bible. Christianity was promised as an era of joy: "In Thy name they shall rejoice all the day, and in Thy justice they shall be exalted".[2] Jesus offered it as an era of joy: "Your joy no man shall take from you";[3] St. Paul commanded joy: "Rejoice in the Lord always: again, I say, rejoice".[4] Nor could it be otherwise. Christianity is a joy in deliverance from the tragic slavery of sin, joy in abundance of life, joy in nearness to God Who is the Fount of joy. A man who does not grasp the importance of joy in his relation with God is not necessarily a bad man. But he is an imperfect one: just as we all are, some in one way and others in another. His idea of christianity is imperfect. He must pray for light. He must live so as to merit light. He must be humble enough to admit that he has more to learn, more to do, more to feel in a spiritual way, before the full beauty of his faith will have begun to reveal itself.

*   *   *   *

The christian life is God's life shared with man. One reason why people can fail to understand that it is a life of joy is that they ignore the human element in it—the fact that it is given to man as his best and highest way of life—and think almost exclusively of some few of the implications in its being given by God, and these not the more fundamental ones.

What I mean is this. Some time or other in the course of a person's life it ought to come home to him that there are ways of life which are more or less satisfying, more or less fruitful in joy and peace. And with this conviction there will come the allied one that God has given him his life to shape and mould according to the pattern of the life which is best

---

[2]Ps. 88, 17. [3]Jo. 16, 22. [4]Phil. 4, 4.

for him. With our whole being, with a kind of substantial passion planted within us in the very act of our creation, we yearn and hunger now for satisfaction and success in life. Misery, which is sheer misery and under no respect satisfying, repels us. Failure, which is unmixed with triumph, makes us shudder backwards in dismay. God did not make us for misery or failure. God did not make us capable of resting complacently—even for a moment, even for the moment of this life—in misery or failure. He made us for happiness and success and, in His great wisdom, made us such that we thirst for the happiness and success for which He made us.

Christianity is the way of life—the all-embracing way of life—which God Who knows our deepest hopes and fears offers us and asks us to accept. In other words, it is the way of life in which we shall find satisfaction and success: it is the way of life in which our thirst and yearning for satisfaction and success are answered. We cannot therefore embrace christianity on God's terms if we ignore that it is going to yield joy. Christianity considered apart from the joy it brings to a man, is a mere abstraction. As well as everything else that may be said about it, it is man's way of life, the life which is best for man, most satisfying, most fruitful, most successful. What possible advantage can accrue from leaving all that out of account? Rather will the result be a failure to cleave with all one's soul to the christian way. The longing for happiness and success which ought to have been converted into an embrace of God, found in the christian way of life, is virtually wasted as a vital energy, and it is with only part of our being that we unite ourselves to Him Whom even the whole of our being cannot encompass.

*   *   *   *

I mentioned a short while ago that too many of us are awake only to what is implied in christianity's being God's gift, and even then to only some of these implications.

It sometimes happens that christianity is regarded as a code of things to be done, with heaven and eternal happiness promised as the reward of its faithful observance. In a certain sense man's longings are left out of this scheme. God commands, God forbids; hereafter God rewards. On earth man obeys: only in the next world does he seem to begin to live what one might call a life. Here his rôle is to know, love and serve. Eternal happiness will follow if he fills his rôle. But what happens while he fills it? The question is hardly asked or answered.

In a general way, of course, those who look on christianity as a way of tending towards God in eternity are quite well aware that even by tending in love towards Him they possess Him already, and that the possession of God cannot be without joy. Their mistake is that they do not make this idea sufficiently explicit. They incline to regard their faith as if it had no bearing on man's innate longing for joy and fulness of life here below. And the result, as has been said, is that they are in danger of putting only part of themselves into their faith: that part of them which even now craves for the best kind of life is given but inadequate attention. All that is desirable is projected into eternity; time is regarded as if given for a striving which yields no immediate results.

There are two ways of growing into christianity, one the copy-book way followed by St. Augustine, the other that of, say, St. Thérèse of the Child Jesus (though I might have chosen instead of her any one of a hundred different saints). St. Augustine's way I call the copy-book way, not to imply that it is the more common, but because it is the more clear, the one in which all the elements involved work in their most obviously logical and uninhibited way.

After an early and incomplete acquaintanceship with his faith, St. Augustine fell into error and sin. There was weakness in that. But there was also zest for life. Even apart from grace he was incapable of settling down into a pointless existence, though he could camp long in a shameful one. There was an emptiness within him he hungered to fill. And gradually it revealed itself as a longing for beauty and for a life which centred on beauty, a longing for that which was most worthy of desire and for a life of filled desire. Pondering thus with himself on his capacity for fulness of life, on his thirst for completion through beauty, he reached God in an ecstasy of desire. The very human fierceness of his desire gave fibre to his life of union with God. He was a man in his quest of happiness, a man in his quest of christianity, a man in his quest of God. And the human in him, ennobled by grace, was the measure of the super-human way of life to which he attained.

St. Thérèse of the Child Jesus—and for that matter, most of the saints—presents a different picture. From early childhood she was sincerely, though not perfectly, united with God. Without any weighing and comparison of ways of life, without laborious thought and effort, she found from the beginning what her heart desired. Her early vocation to the full christian life crystallized into a vocation to Carmel. Into the life of Carmel she grew, finding in it all her heart desired. Not even from its trials would she be gladly freed. They became for her part of the pattern of the fully satisfying life. All this is too obvious, too frequently expressed by her in a thousand different ways, to make it necessary to heap up quotations here. What is of special interest to us is to note that her human longing for God grew under grace. She found Him as a child, and the finding helped her to human maturity. Her longing for God and her joy in Him increased through the years of fidelity to grace, and in that sense the human in her—her human capacity for God—was not so much presupposed by grace as fostered by it. Unlike St. Augustine she found a humanly satisfying life in God without the previous experience of having sought it independently of Him.

There you have the human manifesting itself in two strikingly contrasting ways. St. Augustine, if we abstract from his early inadequate introduction to christianity, came to God, urged and led by a grace which worked through his human desire for fulness of life. He wanted beauty because

in beauty he became alive. And the thirst for life was such
that it refused to be slaked except at the fount of the
Highest Beauty. St. Thérèse, on the contrary, began with
love of God, with tasting that the Lord was sweet. But as
she grew in love so did she grow in capacity for love. As
desire was fulfilled so did desire become unbounded. Tasting
life as a child she became avid of life. Her humanity, we
may say, grew with her grace. In the case of St. Augustine
growth in humanity came first, growth in grace followed.
But for both, the goal was the same: joy in fulness of life.
The one in Carthage, the other in Carmel, found all that the
heart desired, the way of life which was fully satisfying,
fully a life to which a human heart could thrill.

The way of St. Thérèse is, perhaps, the more normal one.
God allows us to start our lives as christians, wishing us to
grow in our appreciation of christianity; not merely in our
appreciation of its obligations, its methods and techniques,
but also in our appreciation of it as our way of life, as the
one way which yields joy both on earth and hereafter. Most
people do this implicitly. Any good christian would consider
it inconceivable to find happiness at the price of his faith.
But there is much to be gained by making this implicit
judgment explicit. Not only is one's adherence to the faith
strengthened, but also the attraction of fair-seeming ways of
life is weakened. We cannot live without joy: we cannot be
good christians without christian or spiritual joy. Bring joy
well to the foreground of your mind. Thank God for His
wonderful goodness in calling you to the way of perfect joy.
Set out in joy to fulfil your obligations. Bear your cross in joy.
Then you are truly, fully living. Then you have resolved the
great problem of life which man can neither escape nor by-
pass without loss.

*　　　　*　　　　*　　　　*

It is the merest commonplace to say that words can affect
people even more than ideas. Theology presents many
examples of this. Take the question of active and passive

virtues. No virtue is so active on man's side as to exclude prior and necessary action on the side of God. No virtue is so passive as to leave man an inert participator in it. Yet the magic of the words "passive" and "active", in complete defiance of the perfectly clear ideas for which they stood, were sufficient to start a minor heresy. We are up against the same difficulty when we speak of man's quest of joy. Many a man does not like the word "joy". Could he be got to say in a single word what he looks for in life he would make use of some very diffierent one—even though on analysis it could be shown to mean just the same thing. I remember a friend of mine who took a most unreasoning objection to the J.O.C. simply because in so many of their manifestos they called on the young worker to be *fier*, "proud". He didn't like the word "proud" and didn't trouble to ask himself what exactly it meant in the context. Likely enough, even were he got to accept the idea he would continue to object to people who used such a word to express it. And so there is need here for a word or two about words. It will be time enough to work on ideas when the question of the words to use will have been cleared up.

"Joy, happiness, pleasure, beatitude, success, achievement, fulfilment, peace", these are some of the stereotyped words we make use of when speaking of a full life. Colloquial or intimate speech provides a number of pictorial expressions: "Feeling you are getting somewhere; doing a worthwhile job; making something out of your life; finding a corner for yourself" and so on. They don't all mean quite the same thing, of course. Broadly, they fall into three groups: words which refer more directly to the thing on which one's life centres; words which refer more directly to one's activity on or in regard to that thing; words which refer more directly to how that activity registers in consciousness. These distinctions may seem a little technical. Really they are quite obvious, and one could hardly pursue the problem of joy without making them at an early stage.

I am keeping in the main to words and expressions which

are in ordinary usage, and have on that account based my division of them on what they refer to more directly, implying that less directly they have other references. The point is that non-technical words tend to cover a lot of intellectual ground whereas techincal ones have a precise delimited meaning. "Doing a worth-while job" clearly refers directly to the thing one is working on, the job one is doing. What it implies is the activity of doing the job and the satisfaction which follows. A man working on cancer research might say he was doing a worth-while job, contrasting his life, perhaps, with that of an acquaintance who spent his time poring over figures in a ledger. And he would have at the back of his head that his work was almost creative and that he got a great deal of satisfaction out of it—the two other points referred to more directly by words and phrases in the other groups. "Making something out of your life" I take, with reservations, to refer more directly to the value of the activity one is engaged in—though the non-philosopher will justifiably find it hard to think of an activity apart from the thing worked on. Perhaps we may put it this way: a life spent in creative work (Don't think for the moment about what is being made) is better in itself than one spent in copying or endless repetition. The creative worker feels he is doing something worth-while with his life: the automaton-like mass-producer, he thinks, is wasting his. Incidentally, of course, the creative worker does imply that he is making something worth-while, and that he gets a thrill out of it. Come now to the words and expressions in the class "joy". They refer in the first place to the conscious reaction to life, to the thrill, exhilaration, deep peace, or whatever it may be, that is got out of life. They imply that the life is centred on something of value and that the activity engaged in is—shall we say?—humanizing. Philosophy and theology can sort out these types of words and the differing ways in which they refer first of all to one thing and imply others much more competently than has been done here. But for our purpose we have gone far enough with this analysis. It now remains to see its bearing on the quest of joy in the christian life.

*   *   *   *

Ask St. Thomas what thing he seeks in the christian life and he will answer "God". You may be surprised, expecting an answer like "peace of soul" or "freedom from sin". Hesitatingly you will agree, feeling the while that he has cheated, that he has left a lot out and put you in a situation where you can hardly protest. After all, you think, what can I seek outside or beyond God. The reason for your hesitation is that St. Thomas, with his clear and almost angelic mind has broken up your question into the parts implicit in it and answered the more fundamental one. He has understood your question in terms of thing, not of activity or reaction. The object round which christianity centres is God, God in Christ. Christianity is, in that very fundamental sense, a quest of God in Christ, a finding of God in Christ, a cleaving to God in Christ. To revert to the unscientific terminology of which we made use a short while ago, God is the "thing" with which the christian life is concerned, that towards which the typically christian activity is directed.

Next comes the question of the christian activity, the doing in which one finds fulfilment. That is, of course, principally, love. Hereafter it will be principally face to face vision. So it could well be said that life is a quest of love which leads to vision, love of God and vision of God. We do commonly say " Look out for opportunities of loving God " as if to remind ourselves that loving God is most worthy of desire. It would be forced to insist on saying only " Look out for opportunities of finding God in love." Both ways of speaking are correct. God is desirable. So also is love and our fulfilment through love. Each is desirable in its own way, God as object or thing most desirable, love as the great worth-while form of activity.

There remains joy. Our acting and doing register in our consciousness. And in that part of it which we call feeling—

which can be spiritual as well as bodily—worth-while
activity, fulfilment in activity, register as joy. Joy is not our
awareness of God nor our love of God. It is our awareness
of being aware of God, our love of loving Him. It is, as it
were, one's deeply personal reaction to life. For him who
fails there is pain or despair. For him who succeeds there is
joy or triumph. There is no one—absolutely no one—but
reacts to life in this way of feeling. The capacity so to react
is a very mark of rational existence. And deep in the core of
such existence is the desire that life's reaction on self may
take the form of joy. The christian wants God, wants to
love God, wants to joy in the love of God. That is the fount
of his quest of joy. He was made for God, made to rejoice
in God. He can find peace only in realizing the purpose for
which he was made.

*   *   *   *

Life is a quest of God, of God found in love, of God
rejoiced in through love. Once more a matter of words—not
everyone warms to the words " joy " and " rejoice." Would
it not be possible to find more acceptable and more expressive substitutes?

In the translations with which we are familiar the New
Testament makes use of many different words to convey
these ideas. In addition to " joy " one thinks immediately of
" peace, rest, life, blessedness, salvation." Every word throws
a peculiar light on some one facet of truth. But among them,
" joy " would appear to be the most expressive, as it is the
most common and, properly understood, it is the full flowering of what all the others mean.

" Peace " and " rest," for example, are at their highest
when they mount up to joy. There is a kind of peace—and
the same is true of rest—which means nothing more than
that conflicting forces have neutralized one another: it is a
stalemate peace, a peace of inaction. We look for more than
that in life: the highest that life has to offer must be
dynamic. And so we rise to the idea of a peace which is

also joy, a peace which is harmonious activity registering as triumphant gladness in our consciousness.

Much the same may be said of " life." Jesus came to give not any kind of life but fulness of life. And with such a life there comes of necessity a sense of exhilaration. One cannot live a full life and know nothing of its thrill.

" Blessed " is much the same thing as " happy " or " joyous "; " blessedness " as " joy." " Salvation " I mention principally because it is a word so lightly accepted in ordinary speech as to convey very little to the ordinary mind. Think of the emotions of one who has escaped from behind the Iron Curtain to freedom. He has been saved, set free. More than liberated from suffering and dread, he has been made an offer of life. That, on the spiritual level, is salvation: freedom from the bondage of sin followed up by freedom to live with God.

Joy is therefore part of the meaning of all these words employed by Our Blessed Lord and His apostles to describe the christian life. If you feel that the word is an unhappy one, with connotations of tiny hands clapping and first primroses and other things, good and innocent in themselves, but too small to appeal to one athirst for life, think less of the word and more of the idea which underlies it. Words can be debased in time, but some at least of them deserve to be restored to their original meaning. Such particularly are those strong, simple and direct words which once bore lightly a meaning under which their weedy modern substitutes crack. " Joy " is one of them. There is a directness about it which is an invigorating challenge. " Joy " obviously stands for a thing which you are going to be for or against. It forces an examination of conscience. And if the examination is honest it starts a quest.

2

JESUS AND JOY

" Despised and the most abject of men, a man of sorrows."
                                                    Is. 53, 3.

THE ultimate test of a way of life claiming to be christian is to examine it in the light of Jesus's example and teaching. How does the idea of a life of joy stand up to this test?

The problem is stated in the clearest terms in the messianic prophecies of the Old Testament. On the one hand there is a group of prophecies which foretell Jesus as joyous even in the sense of trumphant. He is Saviour, Liberator, Victorious King, Glorious Ruler in an era of peace and boundless exultation. On the other, there is the group which speaks of the man of sorrows, and that in terms so detailed and so wonderfully verified in the event as to make one wonder if in Jesus's life there could at any time have been room for joy. Are we to say that the two groups of prophecies caught Him, as it were, at different moments? Not, of course, as if He were a person of changing moods, but as one of contrasting and mutually exclusive experiences.

To answer this question we must take the prophecies in their historical setting. The Jewish people were the people of God, a kingdom that had known glory and shameful decay. God used their history to enlighten them concerning His plan for the future of mankind. In other words, He spoke through the prophets of spiritual things in terms of earthly things that meant much to the people—their past glories, their hopes of a new greatness. Under the images of David and his throne, of Solomon and his splendour, was the spiritual reign of the Messiah, King and Saviour, darkly prefigured. Just as the pagan can pass from the evidence of the world he knows to the existence of God Whom he does not see, so also were the Jews invited in prophecy to pass from the glorious memories of the kingdom they, as a race knew, to the glorious prospect of the spiritual kingdom, they as a race had been promised.

It is significant that the group of prophecies so linked with Israel's past greatness occupies by far the larger space among those which deal with the Messiah. Significant, in that the Messiah is made thereby to appear One essentially triumphant and glorious. He is father, of course, and shepherd, loving and merciful. But He is all that without trace of weakness, all that in the strength of an exuberant goodness which no earthly or angelic power can frustrate. And so, in fact, were the prophecies realized in time. The Messiah Who came was no less a one than God, God with us, and the kingdom He established will have no end. His coming was God's decisive entry into the world. Not as God came to Adam and allowed him to reject Him: not as He came in the Old Testament with but a promise and the shadow of its realization. The Kingdom of Jesus is established to endure: the gates of Hell cannot prevail against it. It is established as the fulness of God's gift to man: in vain would one search outside it for a richer outpouring of grace.

God could not therefore, without falsifying the picture of the messianic kingdom, have spoken through the prophets of it in less glowing terms. But the very splendour of His promises made it all too possible for the Jews to misunderstand them. Their earth-bound minds, dulled by their earth-bound desires, would see less when He offered more; would see an earthly kingdom when He offered a heavenly one; would see a glory of this world when He offered a transcendent one (Do not we also find it hard really to appreciate that the spiritual we do not see is more real and more worth-while than the material we do see?). Hence, while withdrawing nothing of the prophecies that spoke of the glory of the future Messiah, it was necessary that those aspects of His person should also be foretold which would prompt the mind to look for His glory there where it truly was. This, we may well believe, is one of the providential explanations of the second group of prophecies in which the Messiah is depicted as the Man of sorrows, the Man afflicted and despised, the Man Who appeared a failure. The Messiah, it must be held, cannot cease to be joyously triumphant even when sorrow invades His soul, for the prophecies are not contradictory. It is hardly sufficient to say that they are complementary. Perhaps the best way to understand their relationship is to look on one as a fresh divine light thrown on the other, bringing out what the eye did not detect before. How can a triumphant King be a man of sorrows, we ask? And asking the question we see that His triumph is primarily of the spiritual order, His kingdom primarily spiritual. We see the throne of David and the glory of Solomon in a clearer light and we draw from them a richer because a more spiritual meaning.

*   *   *   *

I have begun this discussion of joy in Jesus's life by a brief reference to Jesus in prophecy for the important reason among many that we are deeply influenced in our attitude to the New Testament by what we know of the Old. It would take us too far afield to examine why it is that when we think of Jesus in prophecy we tend, most frequently, to think of Him as the Man of sorrows. But so it is, and that thought colours our whole reading and understanding of His historical life.

At a first glance, it may appear strange that we seem to emphasize most that aspect of the personality of the Messiah which meant least to the Jews and which was practically ignored by them. For them He was to be a figure of glory.

2

For us, He is One Who has suffered. Their difficulty was to see that His triumph was spiritual, ours that His spirituality was triumphant. They, looking forward, could, with reason, see how God promised greatness. We looking backward, see the Son of God throned on a cross. That there should, however, be different view-points is, after all, not so hard to understand. Jesus, in His Person and His life, is a mystery. He cannot be known at all except in the darkness of faith and there He cannot be known fully. Every age will have its own special difficulty in knowing Him, but difficulty there always was and always will be. So it is no wonder that the popular Jewish concept of the Messiah is light where the popular present-day concept of Jesus is shadow. What is important is that we should learn from the errors of the past to strive, under the guidance of the Church, to see Jesus whole, in so far as faith can.

To begin with, turn to the New Testament. Traditionally the mysteries of Jesus's infant years are called joyful. As a young child Jesus would have heard of the tragic events which accompanied His birth and which He was, at the time of their happening, too young to have known experimentally—the massacre of the Innocents, the flight to Egypt, the prophecy of Simeon. But no one ever dreams that this could have made Him a sad, dispirited child. What child could be sad with Mary as mother and Joseph to guard him? The home is the decisive factor in the child's emotional life. Moreover, We may never forget that Jesus could see cause for joy where we, looking at the surface only, can see but pain. He could rejoice in the future glory of the innocent children, in the love and patience and all the other virtues of Mary and Joseph as they brought Him to Egypt, in the heroic generosity with which Mary accepted the sword of sorrow. Even apart from strictly theological consider-ations which we do not consider for the moment, we cannot but regard Jesus's childhood as supremely joyous. And this joy was carried on right down to the beginning of the public life if for no other reason than that all that time Jesus lived with Mary and saw before His eyes the daily miracle of His unimpeded working in her soul.

Coming now to the public life of Jesus, consider first His life up to the time when He began to prepare His chosen disciples explicitly for His impending passion and death. It was a period of great activity in preaching and healing, a period of miracles, and, in the main, of triumphant acclaim. We read here and there of Jesus being weary, of an occasional rejection. But the general picture is one of triumphant progress. There were the faithful disciples, young and eager, to rejoice in; enthusiastic crowds; manifestations of His Father's approval. Jesus was no cynic. He did not despise the spark of generosity that burned in Peter's soul just because he knew Peter would fail Him. Nor did He turn in weary disgust from the thronging multitudes who got so little of His message right. Look on Him as the letter of the gospel paints Him, all consumed with interest in His mission. It is the over-all picture of one who lives a full and intensely satisfying life, one who throws himself without reserve into life. There are, to be sure, deeper mysteries which the over-all picture does scant justice to. But this one fact emerges clear and unquestionable: Jesus's early public life was that of a Man fully living and rejoicing in life's opportunities: one supremely sure of Himself, supremely sure of the direction His life was taking. He is the picture of what one might call the fully-integrated man.

The second part of the public life of Jesus which culminated in His passion and death raises problems which cannot be treated adequately by the simple method of reading the Gospels as biography. Before examining it, however, it is well to pause and see just how much has been established thus far. Nothing less than that the obvious meaning of the story of Jesus's life is that at least up to a short time before His death His life was joyous. You will look in vain in the Gospels for signs of maladjustment, thwarted ambitions, depressions, anxiety, sense of failure and the like. Jesus's attitude to life was one of serene acceptance. Never did He act as if He felt He was born to fail. His life bore the clear imprint of a clearly conceived and fully accepted positive purpose. It was meaningful, satisfying, joyous.

   *   *   *   *

The most wonderful thing about Jesus is that He is God. It is also the key to the problem of joy in His human life.

In His Divine Nature, Jesus, true God of true God, was infinitely and unutterably perfect and happy. No pain of earth could impinge on His pure bliss. Though in Him the Divine Nature was personally united to the human, no doorway was opened thereby through which suffering or loss or lack of any kind might find out His Godhead. As Maker and Sustainer of the world He was sovereignly free from the slightest trace of subjection to the world's influence. His life of Divine knowing and Divine willing, His life within the circle of the Trinity, remained the same life of infinite glory and boundless affirmation after the Incarnation that it had been from all eternity. As God He lived only joy and purest joy.

Jesus was man, truly man, as well as God. He was capable of a fully human life. He had a mind and a will and all the other powers of man. And these He held as one Person, the Same Who was God. Beginning from these truths theology argues to the unique human perfection of Jesus. He could not have becomingly been an imperfect or stunted humanity united in one Person with the Divinity. His human life must, in consequence, have been one of a quasi-infinite fulness which flowered in unceasing joy and exultation. All this is assumed in the doctrine that as Man He had at all times—at all times without any exception whatever—the beatific vision. This beatific vision of His is so important and vital to our understanding of Christian joy that it is necessary to linger a little on the thought, allowing it to sink gradually into the mind.

Modern psychology has made us familiar with the notion of a split personality. A split personality is a defective one and constitutes an obstacle to a full and satisfying life. The same is true of a personality marred by any kind of unresolved conflict or lack of balance and inner harmony. Examples spring at once to mind: cases of ambition which outstrips ability: highly developed mental powers hampered by a weak will or an uncertain sensibility: a great gift for speculation which achieves nothing because of a lack of feel for practical details. Understanding personality in the strict philosophical and theological sense, neither what is commonly called a split personality nor the other type of defects to which I refer here reside in the personality itself: both are more properly defects of nature or of natural powers: it is the mind, the memory, the will, the sensibility which do not work normally.

Now it is clearly inconceivable that any such defects should be found in Jesus. The evidence of facts shows He was free from them. For the Gospels are an historical account of facts and as we see Him in the Gospels He is perfectly balanced, perfectly integrated. Theology, and even common sense enlightened by faith, brings us further. His Personality was Divine, that of the Second Person of the Blessed Trinity. In nature He was God as well as man. What was man in Him had its existence in His Divine Personality and worked in dependence on His Divine Nature. Thus, what He knew as God and wished to reveal to men was grasped by His human mind and uttered by His human lips. What, as God, He willed for man's salvation, was accepted by His human will and executed by His human powers. The human in Him must therefore have been fully attuned to the Divine; else He were unbalanced, at conflict within Himself, a split personality having one set of powers incapable of co-operating in the activities of the other. And in a special way was this true of His mind. His human mind must have been fully capable of entering into the plans of His Divine intelligence. In other words, He must, as man, have read the Divine mind—which is the Divine Essence—in face to face, or beatific, vision. From this, as a consequence, would follow the harmony between His human and His Divine wills.

That is, in modern terms, one of the great theological proofs that Jesus as man enjoyed at all times the beatific vision and was united in will to the Divinity in beatific love. His mind read in vision the mind of God and His will embraced what His mind accepted. Nothing short of such perfection in His human mind and will would have made fully harmonious the union of humanity and divinity in Him in one Person.

Note the consequences of this fundamental truth. Mainly they are that the man Jesus enjoyed at all times on earth the blissful fulness of life that is reserved to the souls in heaven, and did so in the highest possible degree. The moment this is grasped the whole problem of joy in Jesus's life shifts its ground. No longer is it a difficulty to learn that His life was supremely and unbrokenly joyful. The difficulty becomes rather to show that He could have suffered or that He suffered otherwise than in mere appearance. This is a serious difficulty in the sense that it is a great mystery. But it remains possible to throw some light on it.

*   *   *   *

Return now to the Gospel account of the later period of Jesus's public life. We find Him in circumstances in which it has become clear that the opposition of the Scribes and Pharisees has hardened into a hatred that admits of no hope of reconciliation. It has become clear also that the people do not grasp Jesus's message and that their allegiance cannot be fully counted on. The Apostles themselves have not fulfilled their early promise: they are slow to understand, avid of an earthly kingdom, attached to honours, immature and self-reliant. We see Jesus preparing for what He knows will come: He reveals to His Apostles—and how disappointingly they react—that He will suffer and be put to death. Events take their inexorable course. He suffers lonely agony before

His betrayal. He is captured, tortured, put to a most painful and shameful death. He has become the worm and no man, the outcast and rejected. Those tragic days have come which for so many of us, in our heart of hearts, sum up the climax of the christian life, days when life here below seems to mean only pain, frustration and disillusionment, and when the thrill of success and achievement seems finally postponed till that life will have petered out in failure.

A superficial picture, this, of Jesus's last days; a picture which, if true, would call for an entire revaluation of christianity. Its most obvious distortion is that it takes no account of the beatific vision which endured, clear and warming, in Jesus's soul. It views facts on one level only, and those but partially.

It is the nature of the beatific vision that though residing in the spirit it overflows light and joy into the will. Even in the darkest hours of His cruel sufferings Jesus's Humanity was so inundated. His created faculties were, however, capable of receiving impressions in two ways. One, by overflow from above of beatific light and love and joy. The other, in the normal way of contact with His environment. Hence it was possible for Him truly to experience pain even while He experienced bliss. He truly suffered, truly groaned in anguish of heart, truly died. But at the same time He was truly pulsating with fulness of life, truly thrilling to beatific joy. For this joy of His we can offer two explanations. The one, that beatific vision and joy are of their nature perfect and final and incapable of the slightest diminution. The second that Jesus, regarding His sufferings in the light of God's merciful plan for mankind, accepted them unreservedly. He did not rebel against them, breaking thereby His peace and joy of soul. Thus they did not even tend to weaken His beatific union with His Father. While remaining sufferings, and most intense sufferings, they found their place within joy. Jesus is the supreme example of suffering accepted in joy rather than in pain. May we not with justice find that implied in the striking text " . . . Who having joy set before

Him endured the cross, despising the shame . . ." ? [1] What-ever to the validity of this exegesis, it remains true that Jesus's death was an affirmation of life: He laid down His life and no man took it from Him. He laid it down in joy and fulfilment.

*   *   *   *

Though the doctrine of Jesus's uninterrupted enjoyment of the Beatific Vision disposes once and for all of the idea that His life could at any moment have been anything other than sheer joy in living, it is helpful to consider that the same conclusion may be reached by considering His psychology at a lower level and one which is nearer to ours. For it might be objected—unreasonably, as we shall later see—that for us who do not enjoy the beatific vision on earth, joy will never be more than a thing to be hoped for and pain the ever-present fact to be endured.

It is true that the cross will mark every christian life. Pain, disappointment, unfaithfulness of friends and the like are inseparable from human existence. No realistic appraisal of joy in human life, as it really is, rules them out. But a satisfying human life can include them without ceasing to be satisfying. As Aristotle said somewhere, we can be happy, but as men—that is, with the measure and type of happiness which is possible under the actual conditions of human life. What then precisely is it which makes a life happy in spite of pain in all its forms? It consists in two closely allied factors; success in what one has selected as the main all-embracing goal of life and the integration of pain, when experienced, into the attainment of this goal.

Apply these principles to Jesus. The goal of His human life was to establish an order in which God would once more be glorified and souls saved, and this in the manner and measure willed by His Father. To the establishment of

---

[1]Hebr. 12, 2.

that order He devoted His full capacity for life.[2]   It was a work—we speak in human terms—to engender enthusiasm. It amounted to setting the whole world right once more, not only in regard to man in himself and to man in relation to man, but even in regard to man in relation to God. If a high and enduring purpose gives point and value to life, then Jesus's life was clearly the greatest history has known—granted always that He succeeded in its attainment. And that, the first condition of a life joyous in spite of pain, was completely verified in Jesus. His life was a success. He attained what He set out to attain—call it briefly the salvation of the world. Into its attainment He integrated the pain He was called to endure—the second condition for joy. This He did in a way so complete that if pain could cease to be pain it would have so ceased in Jesus's life. For He accepted pain as the means His Father had chosen whereby His life's work was to be achieved. He did not save the world and suffer pain incidentally in the process. He saved the world through love and obedience working themselves out in the aceptance of pain and death. Pain and death were thus introduced into the very heart of Jesus's joy in success, not that they might destroy joy but rather that joy might transform them. Let us be quite clear about this: Jesus's death on the cross was not a failure later made good by His Resurrection and Ascension. His death was a triumph of which His Resurrection and Ascension were the continuation and manifestation, Jesus threw all the ardour of life into His encounter with death just as He had thrown the joy of whole-hearted endeavour into His bearing pain. Death's victory over His mortal frame was swallowed up in

---

[2]His prayer, adoration of the Father and other apparently personal acts fit into this scheme, for in their performance He acted as Head of the human race, and founder of the new order. He did not aim to establish an order as it were outside Himself, for He was its Head and Principle. Hence follows the complete unity of His life-work, unlike that of men who have and cherish interests outside their main one.

His victory over death's attempt to frustrate His work. Thus even on the level where our knowledge of human psychology can throw some light, Jesus's life, apparently marked by failure and sorrow, can be seen to be all success and joy. Not the success and joy that the world knows. But true success and joy, highest success and joy.

The expression " the triumph of failure " is one which comes often to the mind of spiritual writers when treating of the cross in the christian life. What the world regards as failure and feels as failure is often the lot of the christian. It is important for him, therefore, to be armed against failure and to understand how it enters into the christian scheme of things. Still more important is it for him to accept failure in a christian spirit and to work for God rather than for success.

It is natural in this context of thought to look on Calvary as the great failure which proved to be the great success and to seek in union with Jesus crucified the strength needed to struggle on for God in the face of apparently hopeless odds. There is a sense in which this is a deeply christian and heroic attitude. Our Blessed Lord Himself tells us that if we wish to be true followers of His we must take up our cross, the cross of failure as well as every other. But there is another sense in which it is a mistake and may lead to a kind of paralysis which kills or hampers all active effort for the establishment of God's kingdom in the temporal order. It would be tragic were this to happen, for His Kingdom must be established there also. God wishes to rule political organizations, educational works, charitable works, economic planning, scientific progress and the like, not in the sense that these are to be made essentially religious but in the sense that they must be directed in accordance with His Law and thus made contributory to His reign in souls. Those whom He has called to the apostolate of the temporal order may not, therefore, so exaggerate the idea of success through failure as to think and act as if success were a thing to be pursued only half-heartedly. Detached from the thirst for success for his own sake, the active apostle must be attached to it for God's sake and must trust firmly that with God's help it can be achieved. How is this to be reconciled with Jesus's example ?

Jesus Himself worked for a rightly organized temporal order. His efforts were not limited to the establishment of an invisible kingdom within souls. His immediate aim was the establishment of a visible organization, His Church, in which was contained as in its germ, the whole temporal order re-established in Himself. And in that aim He succeeded. He succeeded also in many matters of detail. He did not come on earth to achieve an exclusively spiritual triumph at the price of complete material failure. He came as the Saviour of men living in visible world of space and time and the success of His saving work involved necessarily a measure of visible external success.

The main points in this contention are clear. That Jesus established a visible Church, that He succeeded in doing so, is for a catholic, beyond question. What may not be sufficiently realised is the extent to which He had succeeded at the time of His death. Hanging on the Cross and pondering only the evidence of what He had already achieved, Jesus already knew He had succeeded: His death would seal success. He had given to the world a body of doctrine and had found men who treasured it in their minds. He had prepared a select few to be the pillars on whom His Church would rest, the labourers who would till and extend His vineyard. They were not perfect, but their formation had been well begun: grace would do the rest. He had given to His Church at least some of the sacraments. He had promised the abiding Holy Spirit Who would bring the Church to maturity and guide it throughout all time. He had guaranteed that the power of hell itself would never overthrow what He had done. All this Jesus hanging on the Cross could look on as already achieved. (We are taking for granted that in His beatific vision He could foresee the extent of His triumph in the future.) To speak of His victory in death as a mere triumph of failure is, therefore, an over-simplification that may be a dangerous one. What little justification there is for risking it dwindles to vanishing point if a final point is considered: that standing before His very eyes on Calvary Jesus looked on one who was, for Him, sheer triumph without any admixture of failure, Mary His Mother.

At a certain level—that of merely human affection—Mary's presence on Calvary was an additional source of pain: though even at that level her steadfast love was a source of consolation. But at the higher level of the work He came to do and the doing of which was His life, her presence spelled triumph. For she had understood Him fully, and accepted Him fully, had entered fully into the life He had brought. Mary standing at the foot of the Cross was a figure of His Church, triumphant in face of the assaults of Hell. More than a figure, she was in a sense its reality. In her and in her grace the whole Church at that moment pre-existed, and in her indomitable courage the future Church stood triumphant. Looking at Mary Jesus saw, with His own very eyes, dimmed though they were by suffering and approaching death, that He had triumphed. And saw that triumph in one in whom He had never failed. Jesus on the Cross is not one suffering defeat; Mary at the foot of the Cross does not swoon under an unbearable burden of woe.

In all this no mention has been made of the joy that was Jesus' through the beatific vision. That we take for granted. Neither do we in any way detract in the slightest from the reality of Jesus' sufferings. It ought, however, to be clear by now that the problem of pain and joy, of failure and triumph, in Jesus' life and death admits of no facile solution in the form of four-word paradoxes. " Mors et vita duello conflixere mirando," "Life and death engaged in wondrous conflict." At the very least one must admit that there is something wondrous, something truly mysterious in the relationship between joy and pain, life and death, in Jesus. More than that, one must admit the predominance of joy and life.

The christian life, which is a sharing of the life of Christ, is therefore joyous. Such it was revealed in Jesus' promises which speak of peace, joy, blessedness. Such it can be and ought to be realized in us. Look on the Cross, as you must: live it, as you must. But see there the Victor Who triumphed over pain and death in love of His Father and you; live it as the fount whence life springs, rising unto fulness of life.

3

THE LIFE OF JOY

THREE conditions are verified in a human life which has the fulness that flowers in joy. They are: that it has a worthwhile purpose; that the attainment of the purpose is within one's power; that the purpose is successfully attained.

People have been known to die simply through having no longer anything to live for. Sick people have fought their way back to health because there was something they believed in and which they still wanted to do. We have seen the very physical appearance of a person transformed within a few days of his finding an opening for the development of his talents. And we have often noted the dispirited and listless bearing of those who had drifted into a backwater and saw no hope of making their way out to one of life's main streams.

Even the most unreflecting of us is aware of the importance of having some purpose in life, something worth-while to be achieved or attained. This instinctive conviction is philosophically sound. Our human nature and our human powers have, implanted in them by God, deep longings for expression and realization. These longings are not of the reasoned-out kind that may be argued from one point of view to another or argued even into quiescence. They are part of our very nature and its powers and remain active as long as nature and powers survive. Thus the mind cannot but seek truth, the will seek that which is desirable, the eye seek shape and colour, the ear seek sound, and so on. And deeper than these longings, though of the same kind, is the longing of human nature itself, of the very substance of a man's being, for a self-expression which is also self-development. To frustrate this kind of longing causes a malaise in life which may pile up into misery. While life still lasts the frustration is never complete. A man who is hindered from seeing one particular thing can see others. If he loses his sight altogether he can integrate the loss into his general attitude to life, as must be done with pain in all its forms. Even the deep desire for self-expression and self-development is never utterly frustrated in life: there is no one but finds something he can know and will to do. There is complete frustration of this desire in Hell and nowhere else. But short of complete frustration there are many degrees of approximation to it. The man who has failed, even partially, to give satisfying direction to his life, fails to find full satisfaction and joy. No matter what else he achieves, if in the core of his being there remains an unsatisfied longing, his life is, by human reckoning, a failure.

Does the christian life offer a worth-while purpose?

It offers two supremely imporant purposes, closely connected with each other: that God be glorified and that man be saved. No christian has any doubt that they are important. But seldom enough do we think deeply enough about them to be fully won over to their whole-hearted pursuit.

Do we, for example, believe in a really practical way that to give glory to God is more worth-while than to write a classic or run a service to the moon—admitting, of course, that these things could themselves be done for God's glory? A little reflection is sufficient to convince us theoretically of the supreme value of giving glory to God. The worth-while things a man can do with mind and will and lower powers unaided by grace all fall within the limits of space and time. But man's soul is spiritual. It cannot rest in achievements lower than itself; more than spiritual, it has a capacity for the Divine which cannot be satisfied by the finite and created. Only in an activity which escapes such limitations can it find full expression. Searching for an analogy one thinks of recent advances in the knowledge and use of matter. For centuries matter was known to natural science in the mass only. Then followed the discovery of the molecule and the atom. Each fresh discovery led to new ways of exploiting matter and to new technical achievements. But man was not yet satisfied. The energy with which matter supplied him was still insufficient to produce all the effects of which his enquiring mind could grasp the possibility. Then came the release of the energy stored up in the atom itself, down in the very heart of matter. At once a new era opened up. We are as yet only on its threshold, but we have already caught some glimpse of the extent to which it has widened the scope of scientific achievement.

Grace effects a still more complete revolution. For it enables man to give God supernatural glory and so removes the space-time barrier which limits every other human achievement. It releases man's deepest founts of energy— the atomic energy of the soul. A world in which God is given glory is one lifted out of itself into the divine order. Every act of glory given to God contributes to shaping such a world. Glory does not add to God: it changes the world. By glory this poor limited material world of ours assumes a real if imperfect resemblance to heaven. Whatever is done on earth for God's glory, be it a silent prayer offered in secret or a scientific invention used in accordance with God's law, transforms the world in its appropriate measure, making of it a place wherein God's understanding of its higest potentialities are gradually coming to realization.[1]

Note that glory is not an alternative purpose which can be pursued only by ignoring what is in man and nature.

---

[1]Glory is given to God principally by man's knowledge and praise of Him, but also by every action inspired by knowledge and praise. This idea suggests another approach to the question of the supreme value of the act of glory, namely that such an act utilizes man's powers and the material creation not merely in accordance with their natural potentialities but in accordance with those revealed in them by our knowledge of God and under the guidance of His directing Will.

It is pursued by getting the highest and best out of man and nature and by developing everything else there is in man and nature in harmony therewith. Without glory every human achievement is unfinished. Glory crowns every human work and raises this world to a real participation in the flawless perfection of Heaven.

Thus, in offering to all men the opportunity of giving God glory, christianity does not stifle any worthy human ambition. It does not attempt to force all into the contemplative mould, even though it teaches that charity is the highest act of which we are capable. It encourages the historian to search out the past and offers him the supreme satisfaction of knowing that God is glorified by the truth. It wants the artist to reach perfection in his art, for God Himself is the Supreme Maker. It offers the factory-hand the consoling and vivifying conviction that an honest day's work, even though of a kind that millions do, can be of unique value if God's glory is found in it. Today when so many are confined to work in which there is little or no scope for professional achievement, the importance of christianity for healthy living is, if possible, more important than ever before. God's glory is just the one personal thing left for the average worker to find in his work. Apart from it his work may be soul-stifling slavery. Admittedly, serious attempts are being made to make routine work interesting. These attempts, when wisely directed, are worthy of all encouragement. But the best of them remain within space-time limits. The christian's duty is to adopt their results and raise and perfect them by making of work a tribute of glory to God.

*   *   *   *

The second worth-while purpose which christianity offers is that of contributing to the salvation of the world. It is, perhaps, not sufficiently appreciated that there is a close connection between glory and salvation. In fact, it is only by treating of them in abstraction from real life that one can speak of the one without some reference to the other. Any act of a man which gives supernatural glory to God contributes to the salvation of souls: the soul of the man himself and other souls. Conversely any act of a man which directly or indirectly contributes to the salvation of a soul gives glory to God. We may put the situation this way: the truly christian act gives glory to God and saves souls. The two purposes are not achieved by different acts but by the same acts considered under differing aspects.

Will a man working to save his soul feel that he is doing something worth-while? Is salvation a mere insurance against risk which, when taken out, frees him to devote himself to the joy of living?

To begin with the second question, salvation, unlike an insurance, cannot be taken out and then dismissed from mind. A man saves his soul by making it holy. There is no other way. He saves it beyond reasonable fear of further danger when he makes it as holy as he can. If he deliberately falls short in the holiness he could attain he leaves himself to that extent open to the conviction that he has not made all he might out of his life. God wants us—and we ourselves deep down want the same thing—to save ourselves and others not merely from damnation but also from any deliberate squandering of opportunities. Thus, the idea of salvation does not coincide with that of escaping hell through avoidance of mortal sin: it embraces the pursuit of the highest holiness.

In this concept of salvation is implicit the answer to the other question: will a man working to save a soul feel he is doing something worth-while? Most certainly, provided he understands what it means to save a soul. To save his own soul means to make the best he can out of his own life, first of all in the order of grace and secondly in the order of nature as conformed to grace. To save other souls means to aim at doing the same thing for them. Jesus is Our Saviour. He did not save the world by making it possible for men to balance precariously on the very brink of hell. He saved by making it possible to scale the heights of heaven. To us all Jesus repeats: "If thou didst know the gift of God."[2]

We tend to have a most unworthy notion of what God has given us by making us christians. We think in terms of safety while He offers salvation and look for tranquillizers where He has offered fulness of wide-awake life. Saving a soul is supremely worth-while. No gain can compensate for the slightest permanent loss to a soul.

Every worth-while human activity aims ultimately at widening the scope of human life. There may be artists who profess indifference in regard to the effect their work will have on the mass of mankind. But they claim at least that it gives new dimensions to their own lives and must, in their heart of hearts, hope that it will have the same effect on the lives of perceptive fellow-artists. The scientist does not work for science only. In science he finds for himself a way of life and trusts to find perhaps through it a better way of life for others. What is true of the artist and the scientist is true of every human thinker and maker and worker. No man stops short of mankind in the purpose of his doing. It is all ultimately for man's benefit, all a contribution to man's quest of fulness of life.

Christianity offers man full freedom to do all he can for mankind through his human efforts with, in addition, superadded the completion which grace gives. It enables him to work out for himself and others a way of life which is satisfying in a divine way as well as in a human way. Whatever he can do as artist, or scientist, or ordinary workman, to give meaning to his own life and that of others, all that he will continue to do as a christian with, in addition, the power to add to it supernatural meaning and supernatural energy. True, there are some christians whose vocation is to work directly and almost exclusively for the

[2]Jo. 4, 10.

development of the supernatural. Some devote their lives to practices which are immediately calculated to lead to their own growth in grace. Others devote their lives to a purely spiritual apostolate. These will taste the pure joy of a life fruitful in spiritual growth and detached from the care of adding to human statures. But theirs is the exceptional vocation. Most are called to be christians within the framework of a secular profession or employment. To them particularly does the point made here apply: that christianity offers all of worth-while achievement that the world can, with in addition what only grace can produce. It offers the power to leave a permanent mark on human life, one which will last for eternity as well as for time.

*   *   *   *

Granted that the christian purpose—to give glory to God and to save souls—is worth-while and even the most worthwhile a man can adopt, there arises at once the question: does christianity supply him with the means to achieve it? For fulness of life cannot be found in a purpose, however noble, that is removed beyond one's powers.

A full answer to the question would amount to a full treatment of the machinery of grace with which the christian soul is endowed. It is not necessary to be so detailed here: besides, we have indicated where the answer is to be found. It will be sufficient to refer to a few of the more important points leaving the rest to be filled in on some other occasion.

The christian's capacity to achieve fulness of life resides ultimately in his union with Jesus. "He that abideth in me and I in him, the same beareth much fruit . . . In this is my Father glorified; that you bring forth very much fruit . . . I have chosen you; and have appointed you, that you should go, and should bring forth fruit, and your fruit should remain."[3]

Grace unites one with Jesus Triumphant. Grace is the working in a soul of Jesus' triumph, of the glory He has

---

[3] Jo. 15, passim.

won for His Father and the salvation He has won for men.
Jesus in His earthly life was our model. And the grace He
gives us is a sharing in the grace which was His on earth.
For that reason we are justified in believing that by His
grace we are enabled to reproduce, in union with and in
dependence on Him, the various mysteries of His human
life: there are graces of sharing in His childhood, in His
hidden life, in His life as worker, in His public life, in His
sufferings. He was in all things our model and we, in all
things, are called to live His grace. But it remains true
that every grace He gives us, no matter what the mystery
in which it is a sharing, comes from Him Who is now
triumphant and is a grace of union with Him in His
triumph. Thus the idea of the power to succeed and even
of actual success is included in that of union with Jesus
by grace. Jesus is Victor. In its essence the battle of life
has been won for each of us on Calvary: ". . . this man
offering one sacrifice for sins, for ever sitteth on the right
hand of God, from thenceforth awaiting until his enemies
be made his footstool. For by one oblation he hath per-
fected for ever them that are sanctified."[4] Our perfection
of life is an achieved reality in the power of Jesus Crucified.
In Jesus our fulness of life pre-exists. The christian, united
to Jesus by grace, can find fulness of life, precisely because
that fulness is in Him to Whom he is united. He does not
strain and strive after something outside himself; but life
grows and expands within his soul, he knows not how,
just as happens in the unfailing miracle of the seed. Like
the seed his life is hidden—but with Christ in God, whence
by vital contact it draws increase.

Put otherwise, the christian has the assurance that he
can attain to fulness of life in the simple fact that christianity is a sharing in the life of Jesus. Jesus the great adorer
of the Father, the Saviour of mankind, *is*. To live the life
of adoration or glory and salvation, all that is required is

---

[4]Hebr. 10, 12-14.

to be united to Jesus. It stands to reason that the highest type of life must be one which a man enters into rather than one which, as it were, he builds up by the exercise of his powers. Wonderful though they are, our human powers can never yield anything transcending the human. A life of superhuman fulness and ecstatic joy can be ours only on condition that we turn for it to Someone higher than ourselves. That is why the life we find in Jesus is so full and why all we can do of ourselves is incomplete unless completed through union with Him.

*   *   *   *

When speaking of success in Jesus' life we pointed out that there is no justification for summing it up in the formula "the triumph of failure". Jesus achieved actual success fundamentally in the spiritual order and secondarily in the visible order. Actual success is important for the christian. Without an awareness of actual success his life cannot be fully joyous. It would be obviously unsatisfactory to have a worth-while purpose in life and the means to attain it without any awareness of whether in point of fact one had succeeded or failed. But before discussing the general question of our awareness of success in the spiritual life, it is necessary to examine the more narrow one of the likelihood of achieving actual success in christian works of the temporal order.

There is a mood which finds more to admire in the temporal failures of the saints than in their temporal achievements; failure is thought to provoke sanctity and success to obscure it. St. John of the Cross in his prison seems a nobler figure than St. Theresa achieving a new foundation; St. Bernard after the failure of his crusade appeals more than St. Bernard after the success of his campaign against Abelard. A mood is, of course, no sure guide to truth. But apart from all moods is there not a problem of the relation between success or failure and saint-hood? For the simple fact is that there have been saints who have achieved much in the temporal order and others who achieved little or nothing; saints who have failed conspicuously in the temporal order and saints who failed to do even that.

Is temporal failure necessary? By no means. Original sin did not corrupt nature. The material world of space and time and man's natural capacities are all capable of being used in God's service and for the salvation of souls. It is in God's designs that they be so used. Redemption extended itself even to them. Hence it is that we find Our Blessed Lord establishing a visible organization, the Church, and entrusting to it the continuation of His mission. He did not save men through exclusively spiritual means, but in addition to His invisible grace made use of man's capacity and desire for external organization. He intended to triumph and did triumph in His effort to set up a visible Church. In that intention and that triumph were implicit His attitude to the whole space-time order. He wished to use it all and intended that wish to be realized.

And so we return to the saints through whom His wish was to be realized. How came it that failure was so common in their lives?

Note first of all that nothing attempted in the temporal order for God is ever a complete failure, even in the same order. Pope St. Pius endeavoured to avert the 1914-1918 war and failed. But he left the undying memory of his burning love for peace. He left an example which is also an inspiration. He left to papal diplomacy the guidance of a precedent in times of international crisis which is of value both as showing what can be done and what is likely to fail. And in some measure this last point can be made of any failure: at least it serves as a warning to future apostles, telling them that certain methods are unsuitable or inadequate. That much at least has been successfully achieved in the temporal order: a sign-post has been set up warning away from the road that leads nowhere. It is no straining of words to speak of this as a genuine success; for closing one road often suggests where another may be opened and one man's apparent failure has within it in some way the germ of another's later success. More than that, even in a positive sense, a temporal failure is always, in some measure, a temporal success. Something is always achieved, even if not all that was attempted. It may be left to another to bring to light the germ of well-directed effort hidden in the work of him who seemed to have missed the mark. But that only shows the importance of our aiming always at the implementation of what truly is God's will rather than at what we take to be His will. Paul plants, but does not see the result of his work. Another waters. Neither does he see it. Then comes another who thinks he has noticed a neglected field of labour and under his hand God gives increase. Who among them has failed? No one. What happens is that one enters into the labours of another, one makes use of what remains from the seeming failure of another. And finally something is done for God which would have been for ever undone had there not been those in times past who understood that no failure ever fails utterly and that God's reign in space and time is brought about slowly and by men who are content that the seed of success they planted should be dissociated from their name by burial in the common resting-ground of apparently lost causes.

Why, then, did the saints fail so often? Simply because their failures were in reality the birth of new successes.

There is another reason also for their failure, though, as it is one on which perhaps too much stress is laid, there is no need to elaborate it in these pages. It is that God is wonderfully glorified by holiness and that holiness grows under the stress of apparent failure. Failure helped to empty the saints of self and fill them with God. It brought home to them their weakness and shortcomings and impelled them to turn with greater purity of intention to Him Who is Goodness, Per-

fection and Omnipotence. This is a profound consideration,
easy to express in words and hard to grasp in life. It merits
long and humble examination. But in this present context to
delay upon it would obscure the important point that the
christian may hope firmly to achieve temporal success within
the christian framework. Not, perhaps, success in the precise
form in which he aimed at it. But most certainly success in
some form. On top of that will follow his spiritual success.
And this spiritual success will be not in himself only but also
in those who will be aided to greater holiness by the eventual
penetration of the world by the better order which he had
hoped to set up.

It is most important for an effective christianity that we be
firmly convinced that under God and in continuation of the
work of the Church we can succeed in christianizing the temporal order. There have been moments in history when the
christian seemed to withdraw from the world, believing that
the prevailing order was so corrupt and so strongly established that all hope for the future lay in preserving the
christian spirit and the essence of Church organization free
from its infection. It is for historians to decide to what extent
this withdrawal was complete: on the spiritual level it never
was, for Holy Mass, prayer and meritorious living were
always active as forces to implore God's intervention and
change men's hearts. We, however, do not live in such an era.
God, speaking through His Church, has made clear our
duty to bring the temporal order into line with the plan of
man's salvation by action on the human level as well as by a
vigorous use of our spiritual resources. Thus was the order of
the Middle Ages built up. And if, like all that is human, that
order was subject to decay, the Church has never wavered in
encouraging her children to aim at establishing, each
generation in the form appropriate to it, an order similar in
spirit even if not according to precisely the same formula.
Within our own life-times we have heard the call to restore
all things in Christ—all things, including the temporal,
though these for the sake of the spiritual. Recent popes have

invited christians to play their part in forming a christian social order, in helping medicine and science to find their true place and at the same time their true line of development within God's plan for mankind. Such invitations are divine guarantees that success is possible. The Church invites us to attempt the difficult, not the impossible. God wants the Church to succeed in the world. She too wants success. We who love God and His Church want to succeed in what we attempt for her. Would not christian joy be deprived of its fulness were not actual success in spiritual-material enterprises one of the christian's unquestioned hopes? In a very true sense we need more interest in success, not less. There is a false detachment from visible results which takes the heart out of effort. Masquerading as respect for the supremacy of the supernatural, it is in truth a form of despair in the power of the Redemption to save the world.

*   *   *   *

The greatest paradox of the active christian life is that visible results are the fruit more of invisible holiness than of visible efforts. And the paradox is so striking that spiritually-minded men often find it hard not to exaggerate it into an absurdity.

Most spiritual books avoid this exaggeration. There are classics on the primacy of the spiritual of which one would hesitate to alter a sentence. But readers can and do misunderstand. We may meet religious of a contemplative turn of mind who only barely believe in the value of the work of an active priest or social worker. They are, of course, completely wrong. But their position is plausible enough to raise doubts in the minds of active christians and take something from the joy their work for God ought to yield. Contemplation is not activity's rival. True contemplation understands that action is necessary just as true action understands that without charity —which is the core of contemplation—it is valueless. Within the Mystical Body both the contemplative and the active have their place, just as within the span of Jesus' life on earth time was found for prayer and action. Those whose vocation is action need prayer in their own lives and the support of the prayer of contemplatives. A contemplative who refuses that support lacks charity. His contemplation is an illusion and a selfish one.

*   *   *   *

The purpose of the christian life on earth is not primarily to establish christian institutions but to extend the empire of God's grace in souls. Herein lies the value of institutions: that they favour birth to the life of grace and growth in it. Hence the christian's deepest joy springs from success in his efforts to grow up in Jesus through grace. Without this growth no success in externals can yield genuine christian joy. To what extent can the christian be aware that he has succeeded in attaining close union with Jesus?

The Council of Trent teaches that no one can be sure, with that special certainty which is peculiar to faith, that he is in the state of grace. In other words, my personal holiness here and now is not one of the things revealed by God and proposed by the Church infallibly for my acceptance. This does not mean, however, that a christian must remain in doubt about the condition of his soul, but rather that his knowledge of it comes otherwise than by the way in which he knows that there are three Persons in God. God has revealed to us through His Church what are the normal means of acquiring and growing in grace and what are the more usual signs of His friendship. These truths are known by faith. By applying this revelation to his own case a person can know with moral certainty—which means a certainty that leaves no room for founded doubt—whether or not he is in the state of grace. Thus he knows by faith that the Sacraments are the normal causes of grace and of increase in grace. He knows also the dispositions with which the sacraments are to be received. He knows what is mortal sin. If he examines his way of life in the light of such truths of faith he will arrive at a morally certain judgment that he has received grace and growth in grace through the sacraments, or that he has lost grace through mortal sin. His judgment is not itself faith, but one resting on faith. It is certain with all the certainty a man needs, without having the special certainty only faith can give.

A person who is leading a good christian life does not, however, normally examine himself in this precise way, no more than does a person who feels in good health try to make sure of his condition by frequent self-applied tests. As St. Augustine so beautifully puts it, the soul has its own joys deeper than the joys of the senses. There is a joy in doing good, a joy in being in God's grace, a joy in union with Jesus, which is itself an assurance that one's life is spiritually successful: not, of course, an assurance of faith, but one which engenders moral certainty. "For the Spirit Himself giveth testimony to our spirit, that we are the sons of God. And if sons, heirs also; heirs indeed of God, and joint-heirs with Christ . . . .".[5] This is the pleasure in divine things and the zeal for the salvation of souls which theologians give as signs that one is in God's grace. With such signs, and the conviction based on regular humble examination of conscience that one is not guilty of mortal sin, there is no need to pile up arguments to prove that one is in the state of grace. Grace is life. Somewhat as life in man is accompanied by awareness of life, so also is grace accompanied by awareness of grace: not an awareness through vision, not an awareness through faith, but an awareness through peace and joy. Christian peace and joy are spiritual success welling up to the level of consciousness: they are the thrill of achievement without the vision of what has been achieved.

And so we conclude that the christian life verifies all the conditions necessary that it be capable of yielding joy: it gives life a worthwhile purpose; it gives the assurance that the purpose can be attained; it admits of the conviction that it

---

[5]Rom. 8, 16-17.

has been attained. In regard to the second point we have lingered over the question of success in the temporal order more than that of success in the order of grace. The consequence has been an inadequate treatment of the joy which follows from union with Jesus. Later chapters will make good this disproportion. For the present it is enough to have shown that joy is the lot of both Martha and Mary. Wherever there is a hunger and a thirst for justice, there is joy.

4

VIRTUE AND JOY

CONTRARY to what is so often said, our childhood days are not the happiest of our lives. Childhood is the time when a man is least fully alive and least happy; normally, one must add, because of the men who fail to grow up and the men who shrivel with the years. In childhood a man's capacity for appreciating and doing the things that count is slight. Hagiography tells us of exceptions to this rule. But even among saints the rule held for the majority: they grew in sainthood, and even when saints as children became still more saints as grown men.

A child's first experience of joy on the truly human (as distinguished from the more or less animal) level begins with the awakening of its first intelligent interest. Up to a certain age all things are more or less the same to the child. Their purpose is to be chewed, taken to bits, thrown about. Something of the same fundamentally selfish indifference persists during the early years, broken only according as things cause pleasure or pain. Then comes the significant change. One day, a thing, a type of thing, is found to be interesting in itself. It may be a plant, an animal, a mechanical toy, a doll. The child begins to be absorbed. Working on or being with its thing gives joy, which is an experience of a higher order than pleasure. And as they develop, there comes a time when children begin to see something apart in their parents, something that draws them and inspires them to act in a certain way. This, when it happens, is more than just to come to the age of reason. It is to come to the age of an enlightened reason, to have laid hold on an idea that will help to determine the course of life and open up invaluable possibilities of rewarding unselfishness.

Such simple facts of human psychology help to explain the scholastic doctrine of habit and virtue.[1] We are born into this world soul and body, powers of soul and powers of body. In all these departments there is room for development. The soul may remain on the natural level or be raised by grace to a sharing in the divine nature. The body may weaken under disease or grow strong and healthy. The powers of the body may be trained to more sensitive and effective use, or may be neglected. The same holds for the powers of the soul—the mind and will. The scholastic way of saying this is that in the course of time and as a result of how we act, certain habits are added to or acquired by our powers, channelling their use in one direction or another, making us act by preference one way rather than another. Those habits which channel our powers in a worth-while direction are called virtues. Those which channel them in the opposite direction are vices. Grace which perfects the soul itself, and health which perfects the body, are in a special category which does not concern us just now.

Before passing on from this brief explanation of virtue, it will be helpful to recall the derivation of the word "virtue" itself. Scholastic philosophers looked, with reason, on derivations as one of the roads to understanding things: one word links up with another just because things do the same. "Virtue" comes from the Latin *"vir"* meaning "man". It is a pity that ordinary usage does not allow us to say that virtue is a manliness, for that is just what it is. Not "manliness" which has its own meaning already, but *a* manliness, a way of

---

[1] We are concerned here only with those habits—called virtues—which are immediately connected with action. Sanctifying grace is a habit which perfects the very essence of the soul and is, therefore, of a different kind from those which perfect the soul's powers of acting.

being manly, a quality of the type that goes with developed manhood. In other words, virtue is immediately connected with human life and fulness of human life. The more virtuous a man is the more he is alive. Virtue has nothing whatever to do with namby-pamby listlessness. A virtuous man has a sharp thirst for life, a keen sense of what life is and what is the value of life, a more than ordinary energy and determination in getting the most out of life. Quite simply he is more a man than others are who are less virtuous: he has got further than they along the road from undeveloped childhood to manhood's full stature. His powers of soul and body have an added energy not found in those who have not his virtue and this energy is his to throw into the adventures of life.

*   *   *   *

Even a slight acquaintance with the great Aristotelian philosophy of virtue as developed by the scholastic thinkers is sufficient to convince one of the amazing range of the virtues which perfect man's powers. Some are acquired by repeated actions. These are the natural or acquired virtues and have no intrinsic connection with the life of grace. Such for example are the virtues of pagans who in the course of their lifetime grow in justice, truthfulness, respect for authority, knowledge of branches of science and the like. Higher than these are the specifically christian virtues which are conferred on the soul with sanctifying grace: faith, hope, charity, supernatural prudence, justice, fortitude, temperance and so on. These virtues are known as "infused" since they are, as it were, poured into the soul by grace. Though not acquired as a result of repeated acts, their development depends on their use, and under that respect they are akin to the acquired virtues. And since grace is built up on nature, their development depends in part also on the development of the natural virtue corresponding to them. For example, respect for parents as sharers in God's paternity in the order of grace does not normally develop without respect for them as the authors, under Him, of life in the natural order. And this is one of the reasons why, in spite of having the infused virtues, christians may fall in the time of temptation: their foundation of natural virtue is weak and that weakness contributes to causing the edifice of infused virtue to topple.[2]

We have already seen that christianity does not stifle manhood: all that is good in man can be taken up into the order of grace and there given its full development. Grace adds to nature: it does not destroy it. For that reason it is not necessary to show in detail how the exercise of all the virtues, both natural and infused, leads to fulness of life and joy. Among the virtues there are, however, some which are of special importance. These are faith, hope and charity. Our immediate concern will therefore be to show how life of faith, hope and charity is joyous. A few other virtues will be considered after these three because of special points of interest which they offer.

*   *   *   *

Faith, St. Paul tells us, is " the substance of things to be hoped for, the evidence of things that appear not".[3] Hence its importance. For the highest in christianity are the things not possessed in this world, things to be hoped for and which do not reveal themselves to unaided reason. And since christianity is the highest life open to man it follows that faith is necessary in order to achieve true success. Faith is, in other words, a virtue in the sense in which we have explained the term. It is a quality, an endowment, added on to one of man's powers—the mind—and endowing it with a new energy to grasp the meaning of life and to see how to exploit it fully.

Faith tells us first of all about God—He Whom we hope to see and Who as yet appears not—and then about ourselves and all other things in the light of their relation to God. It enables us to accept on God's authority and from the lips of His Church the revelation which He made of

---

[2]Obviously this is a very summary treatment of the manner of growth of the infused virtues and, in another context, would need considerable amplification.

[3]Hebr. 11, 1.

4

Himself and His creation in Jesus. It makes us to know the things which are of vital importance for a deep understanding of life. Without faith we should remain on the surface of life, seeing what is obvious and the relatively unimportant in it, but missing all that is of enduring value.

When therefore a man accepts on faith a truth regarding God or the Church or his own soul and the meaning of life, he performs an act rich in content beyond the understanding of any truth of natural science. True, faith is not vision: we do not see into the heart of what God reveals, whereas an able scientist can see far, even if not all the way, into the heart of matter. But the imperfection inherent in faith's manner of knowing is more than compensated for by the sublime perfection of what it knows. God known by faith answers to a deeper longing of the mind than does matter known by reason. And because faith is God's answer to a deeper longing, so the exercise of faith engenders a deeper joy. Just to think about God, to turn over in one's mind what faith tells of Him, is a thrilling intellectual experience. And there is all the rest of revelation to think about also—Jesus, Mary, the Church, the love, the mercy, the goodness of God. Why do we so often miss the thrill? For one reason, because we do not appreciate the value of an act of faith. A mathematician whose heart is set on music gets very little satisfaction out of solving mathematical problems. We are often in a similar situation. Though first and foremost christians, our hearts are set on satisfactions outside of christianity. With so many things to think about we turn to God only through a sense of duty and then without expecting to find Him interesting. Were there more humility in our faith there would be more joy in it. Did we think more of the privilege it is to know God revealed to us in His own words, humble gratitude to Him would open the way to joy.

Faith corresponds in a special way with the first of the three conditions required for a successful life: that it have

a worth-while purpose. For it is faith which reveals the
high purpose of the christian life. Through faith we get our
first inkling of all that life can be. It shows that life has
more dimensions than those of space and time. And doing
so it brings into life an exhilarating sense of freedom. It
tells us that we are not confined within the limits of this
visible universe, but that the road to the Infinite is open
and inviting before us. It shows us an unending and inex-
haustible possibility of joy and growth in joy which makes
life a new opportunity of thrilling fulfilment. Even if he
fails to live by it, the man who has the gift of the faith
sees life in terms of greatness. That vision, contrasted with
what he is making of himself, fills him with deep unrest.
Conversely, the vision of life's greatness is the beginning
of the true christian's joy. Seen in the light of faith, even
the most commonplace type of existence is transformed into
significance. Faith makes a man all the more a man by
showing him a way to perfect manhood whatever his circumstances of birth and fortune, of place and age.

*   *   *   *

The second condition for a successful life is that it be
one with an attainable purpose. A life with a dream-goal
which can be thought of but never attained is, perhaps, better
than one with no goal at all: but it remains no more than
the pale shadow of a life whose goal is real and really
attainable. Hope is the virtue of the attainableness of the
goal of the christian life.

Christian hope is a kind of reliance: not self-reliance,
but God-reliance. There must be some kind of reliance
in life if it is to escape despair. In matters of daily life
most people rely on themselves. They feel they can manage
the ordinary things that usually crop up—work, domestic
affairs, social relations and the like. The feeling gives a
certain tranquillity to life, a certain feeling of sureness
which is a type of joy. To lose that self-reliance means fear,
insecurity, unhappiness.

Hope is a reliance which is founded on God. It is the implanted, or infused, assurance that one has God to count on for making life a success. It is not a feeling in any sense of the term. But it occupies a place in our supernatural psychology corresponding with that which feelings do in our natural psychology—in particular, the feeling of confidence. It is confidence in God: trust in His infinite power and His capacity to turn all things to our good; trust that His Power is with us by grace, that every grace of action He gives us is a sharing in His strength. Thus, hope is a reliance which knows no limit. Self-reliance, if it is to be reasonable, must know a limit: there are things a sensible man knows he cannot do and yet may be called on to do. Not so our God-reliance. Whatever we are called on to do in the attainment of our full supernatural stature can be done by God in us. And that is as if we were to be able to do it of ourselves. For God is our Father, abiding in us and making us to abide in Him, making common cause with us in the business of life, giving us already here on earth a child's share of His Infinite knowledge in faith and a child's share of His Infinite Power in Hope.

Hope, of course, does not replace that natural self-reliance which it is only right and proper for a man to have in the ordinary matters of daily life. It is right and proper to feel that my powers of body and mind will continue to function as they have functioned in the past and that the skills I have acquired will be mine to use as long as I do not allow them to die through lack of practice. Hence a person does not call immediately on the virtue of hope to assure him that he will be able to read the paper or prepare the breakfast. Even though ultimately these things do depend on God, we know that He respects the natural powers He has given us and provides for their normal functioning as a matter of course. Hope enters in primarily for matters which are above the normal functioning of a man's powers, for matters which concern the achievement of his supernatural destiny. This it does by assuring him that in undertaking them he can rely on God's Power as if it were his own. It is, therefore, the foundation of our specifically christian optimism. It is the conviction that the future holds our true good and what can be turned to our good. Above all else, it is the conviction that eternal success, the success for which man as man experiences the deepest longing, is possible with the help which God, Our Loving Father, refuses to none of His children.

St. Paul associates joy in a very particular way with hope. In hope we are saved,[4] in hope we ever rejoice.[5] It is only natural that christian joy should rest not on the past nor the present, but on the future. Joy works from the future, from eternal joy, back into the present. The future holds our true fulness of life. The life that passes with the body and that is bounded by time is but a part, and by far the lesser part, of life. We are made for eternity and our joy rests primarily not on the spiritual success which now is, but on the unending success which is to come. This does not mean that our life in time is of negligible importance. In time is planted and watered and given increase the life that matures in eternity. But life's full development is for hereafter. Hence, the chief function of hope in regard to life here below is to assure us that with God's help it will never cease to tend positively and vitally to eternal fulness of life. It guarantees that God will see us through the time of weak beginnings. In that guarantee there is already joy. But a further joy is ours also. For in regard to fulness of life, hope assures us even now that it is possible with God's help. This assurance is an anticipated tasting of eternal joy and brings into mortal life something of the finality of complete achievement. It brings God's unchanging peace into the to and fro of the daily struggle. It casts out fear and insecurity and enables us to find that serenity which

---

4Rom. 8, 24.
5Rom. 12, 12.

is necessary in order to live and work wholly for God in a world so often turned against Him.

*   *   *   *

Faith is acceptance on the Authority of Another: Hope is reliance on the Power of Another. Is it not strange, incomprehensible even, that peace and joy can spring from something which is not a man's own but which he holds at another's will?

There is a mystery here, but it is the mystery of man himself rather than of his faith and hope. Man comes from the hand of God an unfinished being. He is given a beginning of life to which the finishing touches are yet to be applied. And this beginning of life is itself so perfect that its possibilities cannot be exhausted by any process of mere self-development. Nothing that a man can make out himself by himself or with any created aid is all that he can be. Nothing that he can add to himself by the enrichment of his human powers of soul and body through their exercise on the universe in which he finds himself will bring him to his full stature. He becomes all that he is capable of only when he allows himself to be caught up in the fulness of life and being of Him Who Is. Man is made for the highest perfection. And the highest perfection is not a state built up from human resources in the course of time. It is union with a Being Who is from all eternity and in Whom perfection pre-exists, inviting man to enter into its possession.

It is, of course, true that ultimately we cannot even conceive of a creature whose happiness springs from the exercise of powers that are exclusively his own, for the simple reason that every creature holds all that it is and does from God. But this is not the point we are making here. Our point is that even granted certain powers given him by God and granted also their normal exercise, man cannot find his full perfection and development in them alone. For in the very nature of things a finite being perfecting itself by the progressively improving exercise of its powers over a limited stretch of time can never arrive at anything more than an essentially limited goal. Only by stepping outside the finite into the infinite is one reached beyond which there remains nothing to desire. To describe this process as "stepping" is an obvious inaccuracy. A man cannot step from the order of what is within his powers into the order of what exceeds them: he can only be lifted. For man to transcend the life which his unaided powers open up to him, God, to Whom belongs by nature the order of the infinite, must draw him unto Himself. Hence, only through God's gratuitous love and mercy can the full capacity for perfection and joy He has given to man be satisfied. Without God's special intervention he can, of course, develop as man and be happy as a man can be. But the more-than-that of which he is capable becomes his only when he surrenders himself to God in Whom subsists all fulness of life, at once Divine and supernaturally human.

Life on earth is a real sharing in and anticipation of fulness of life in heaven—for grace is the seed of glory. Here on earth the christian is lifted from the order of the finite to that of the infinite. He moves towards the perfect life of heaven by allowing himself to be taken up gradually into God's life on earth. God and His life and His joy enter into the soul at different levels. Deepest down is the level of sanctifying grace and Inhabitation whereby the soul is endowed with a share in the divine nature and the Three Divine Persons communicate Themselves, as it were to its very substance, whence to overflow into its powers. Next follows the level of intellect and will. Into the intellect flows the light of the God of truth, not in all its brilliance but dimmed and veiled; yet so truly that when we accept an article of faith we do so in virtue of the mind's limited natural capacity but with a certainty which derives from God's own grasp of truth. Into the will flows first of all the power of God, not in all its fulness, but as working in us by grace which leads to glory. And that is the presence which makes hope exultant. Into the will flows also the goodness, the attractiveness of God, to be seized by the virtue of charity in the least veiled encounter of any the soul has with God on earth.

Of charity we shall speak shortly. In regard to faith and hope, we can now point to a second source of their fruitfulness in joy. It is that they set us in contact with God as their motive even more than as their object. By faith we know God and the things of God dimly. That is faith's object, and a source of pure joy. But faith's motive brings us even nearer to God. Its motive is God Himself, the Source of all truth. By faith we believe on God's authority, that is, on God Himself as vouching for the truth of what His Church teaches. Across the Church's formulae moves the God of truth, leading us to acceptance, and our acceptance is a response to living contact with Him: a response which involves a thrill of joy, for how otherwise could the mind respond to contact with Subsistent Truth? [6] In a similar way hope establishes contact with God both as object and motive. The object hoped for is God to be possessed for all eternity: the motive is the even now present power of God Himself Whom we do not yet possess in vision. Faith and hope do not, of course, yield their full quota of joy unless they are crowned by charity. For it is through charity that our union with God is finally sealed with loving reciprocity. Without charity, faith and hope set us in contact with the truth and power of a God from Whom we are otherwise separated. But even then they do not cease to be fully theological. Nor do they fail to add to man's stature. The sinner who has held on to faith and hope, either or both, is more than the pagan who has neither. There is a

---

[6]Contact with God as the object of faith is, of course, not the same thing as contact with Him as the motive of faith. The object is "what" we believe; the motive is the ultimate ground for belief. In other words, the object is believed on the ground of the motive. Hence there is in faith a double contact with God: one with Him as the veiled object of faith; the other with Him as the unperceived but vitally present motive of faith.

light in his mind, however dimmed by sin, and a strength in his will, however weak otherwise, which belong to the order of the infinite. In his faith and his hope he has manlinesses or characteristics of developed manhood, incomparably superior to the best in an unbeliever. There remains but the tragedy that having so much he should cling by sin to so little.

* * * *

There remains charity. Charity fills an anomalous role in the christian life. As a virtue of the will it ought, one should have though, to rank after faith, the virtue of the mind. The condition of human life, however, necessitates that among the theological virtues this order be reversed. The life we know is a movement towards God, a time when we allow ourselves to be drawn by Him. Priority belongs therefore to the virtue by which we turn towards Him as our goal and submit to the attraction of His grace: that is to say, to the virtue of love or charity. Full possession of God is not for this life: only the dim contact of faith is granted to the mind on earth. The mind functions therefore in an imperfect way on earth and for a time must yield pride of rank to the will. Of course, not even the will's absorption in God can be full during life. But however imperfect its absorption, charity's object is God Himself, not His dim image. Put otherwise, our love goes out immediately to God Himself whereas our knowledge of Him is a mediated one which is uttered and acepted in the created word of revelation. Thus it is that charity establishes closer contact with God than faith does. Not as if the will became through charity a possessive faculty, but rather because love as such abstracts from presence and absence and having God in Himself as object may in a sense be said to make Him present even before He withdraws the veil from His face.

It is important at this point to clear up a possible misunderstanding. Charity does not love an absent God and by its intensity create an illusion of presence. God is not absent from the soul in the state of grace. He is intimately present to it. In Him we live and move and have our being. He abides in us and we in Him. The function of the theological virtues is simply to enable us to establish contact with Him Who is really present in our souls; to taste and see that the Lord Who dwells within us is sweet. Faith tastes Him only imperfectly as object, but more intimately as motive, as Subsistent Truth. As object, hope tastes Him only as One Who is yet to be possessed in vision; as motive it contacts His Power, Which is Himself. Charity, however, contacts Him both as object and as motive. As object, for charity is love of Him Himself Who dwells in the soul; as motive, for it is His loveableness, His goodness —which is Himself, the Supreme Good—that attracts the soul. Thus faith, hope, and charity all bring God into the psychology of daily life by being so many different forms of sensitivity to His fully real presence and action within the soul. And among the virtues charity does this most completely. It alone is sensitive to His Divine Reality Itself both as object and motive: faith and hope are imperfect in their openness to Him as object, faith admitting Him to the mind only in the mirror of revelation and the darkness of the concepts of which it makes use, and hope admitting Him to the will only as One not yet but one day to be possessed.

By love we drink deepest from the torrent of the joy that is God. To love Him involves joying in Him. To love our neighbour for His sake is once more to joy. Every act of love releases something of the uncreated torrent of joy that dwells within our soul. And our will, which was made for God, exults to find itself laid hold on by Him for Whom it longs.

*　　　*　　　*　　　*

In addition to the theological virtues there are the infused moral virtues and the gifts of the Holy Ghost, all of which in their functioning bring joy into the christian life. From what has been said already about virtue in general, the way in which this is done by the moral virtues will be clear. Prudence, justice, fortitude and temperance are all super-

natural perfections of man's powers. As such they give him
an additional capacity to grapple with and wring success
from life. Their exercise is a kind of triumph, a victory
won over the world. It is therefore accompanied by joy, as
is every act of a man by which his manhood gains increase.[7]

The gifts of the Holy Ghost however deserve somewhat
more detailed consideration. For they are given us by God's
love precisely in order that our christian lives may be
marked by the peace and sureness of a child moving and
acting within its own family circle.[8] To understand them we
must start from the fact that God's grace and the infused
virtues are received into our souls in an imperfect way.
Grace is nothing less than a sharing in the Divine Nature;
the infused virtues are so many shares in God's wonderful
perfections. Human nature and our human powers are
immeasurably below grace and the virtues. So far below
are they, that when we have received them and are raised
to the divine order by them, there exists something of a
conflict or a disproportion within us: our poor nature and
our limited natural powers—weakened, it must be added,
by original sin—are slow to respond to the deifying influence of grace and the virtues. By nature mere men and by
sin fallen men, we cling sluggishly and stubbornly to our
gross condition.

In His love God provides a remedy such as a father or
mother provides for a child. When a child sets about its

---

[7] I pass over the more theoretical questions of the relationship
between the acquired and the corresponding infused moral virtues
as well as the precise way in which we gain facility in the use of
these latter, neither of which affect the general argument outlined
above.

[8] This is the explanation of the Gifts given by St. Thomas in the
1a 11ae, Q 68, a 2. I have developed it at greater length in "The
Seven Gifts of the Holy Ghost", Sheed and Ward, London and New
York. Many theologians prefer the explanation St. Thomas gives in
his commentary on Isaias, a work in which he had not reached the
theological maturity of the Summa. This explanation is, however,
open to serious difficulties.

first attempt to write, we do not say: "You have a mind and a will and a hand and a pen and a headline. Begin right now". It is true that the child has all the powers mentioned. But it has only a very imperfect control of them. It needs help in their use. And so we guide its hand in the beginning, and do so very lovingly when the child is our child.

We have grace and faith and hope and charity and all the other virtues. But, being what we are, we are not at home with them. Armed with virtue we are as unhappy as was David in Saul's unexceptionable armour. So God comes to our assistance. He guides us in a specially helpful way in our thoughts, words and actions: so helpfully that we come to think, speak and act as if to do all that in a truly christian way were natural to us—which, of course, it is not. Our loving God—the Holy Ghost—helps us to behave as born members of God's family (Though often enough we refuse His help or accept it while half-resisting). He makes us feel at home in His love and service, gives us a kind of instinctive appreciation of what is expected of a member of God's family living for the moment in exile on earth. The gifts are simply the channels through which this help is communicated to our souls: they are given to make us receptive of the Holy Ghost's special loving help.

Without examining the different gifts in detail it is at once clear how much they all contribute to the joy of the christian life. They make us at home, and make us feel at home, in christianity. Being made a christian is rather like getting unexpected promotion for which you are poorly prepared. You will be ill at ease and groping in your new post unless someone has the charity to lend a helping hand and steer you through the first few weeks. With a helping hand the promotion becomes a wonderful chance: without it it could be a dangerous risk. Taken by Baptism from among God's enemies and made His child, the Holy Ghost abides with us to help us through the testing days of this life. With Him at our side the christian life becomes a reassuring and friendly challenge to reach the top of the ladder of grace.

* * * *

Among the Gifts of the Holy Ghost the gift of Wisdom is of special importance. It is the gift of the christian outlook, the christian mind. As such it colours one's whole reaction to life.

Everyone, even the most unphilosophical, has some kind of a general attitude—or it may be a complex of more or less general attitudes—which has a great deal to do with adjustment to life, with success or failure in it, with joy or discontent. There are enterprising people of fair ability who take difficulties in their stride, and diffident men of genius who are always pulling out of something or foreseeing the time they may have to pull out. There are people who feel they can manage anything and others who are afraid they can get nowhere. These, of course, are simple cases, drawn in contrasting black and white. But they are true enough to life to make the main point clear: that the joy or misery a man finds in life depends in great measure on his attitude quite independently of whether circumstances are in themselves favourable or unfavourable to him.

By the gift of wisdom the christian sees life in terms of God's loving Fatherhood of man. We know by faith that God is Our Father and that He takes loving care of us by His Providence. But this truth is so much above the ordinary level on which we analyse life that without special help from the Holy Ghost it is likely to remain unnoticed at the back of our minds. The Holy Ghost brings it right to the forefront of consciousness—and that in a habitual way—by the gift of Wisdom: and links up charity with faith in the process, since it is a loving eye which sees things in such a light. Wisdom makes us at home with God, showing us that He is Love, showing us His love in Jesus and Mary and in the

whole machinery of salvation. It makes us at home with
this ragged and unpredictable world, revealing it as the
home of God's children and the centre of His loving care
of the universe. It makes us at home with our fellow men,
all of them called to God's family life, as we are; weak, as
we are; sustained by their Father's hand, as we are. It
makes us at home with ourselves, made what we are by
the grace of God, a grace that has not been in vain, and
relying for what we must yet be on the same grace and
on the loving Father from Whom grace proceeds. That is
the wisdom of the christian, a wisdom that looks foolishly
childish and immature to the world. It covers the whole of
life. It clothes everything in supernaturally reasonable
optimism. It may seem to have its limitations. For example,
it has little to say about the scientific secrets of outer space,
though it does tell us that it is part of God's domain and
that His care and His law extend there. It has little to
say about the psychology of the subconscious, though it
assures us that the man whose subconscious is being
investigated is God's child. But just because Wisdom is
so little concerned with the universe on its ordinary or
natural level, and so much with the Father of light, from
Whom is every best and perfect gift,[9] it is a complete
philosophy of life for every man, no matter what his calling
or profession, provided only he is willing when handling
this world to respect the broad structural lines given it by
its Author and included implicitly in our loving recognition
of Him as our Father in Heaven. Wisdom is as relevant to
the life of the atomic scientist as to that of the cloistered
religious or the homeless refugee. All live in the same world
which comes from God's hand and is ruled by His Providence—a world in which nothing happens to them that is
irrelevant to their spiritual growth or is unaccompanied by
the grace to turn it to good. The pattern of their lives is
different. The stuff is the same: the love and service of

---

[9]cf. James I, 17.

God sought with the help of God's love and guidance in laboratory, cloister or refugee camp. Wisdom sees the Father behind the setting of one's life. And seeing Him we are at peace.

* * * *

With the Gift of Wisdom one may associate the purest of the joys which spring from the exercise of the virtue of charity, joy in God and in His infinite perfection. Love of friendship, when it is pure, rejoices whenever the one loved has reason to rejoice. That is what is meant by "congratulating" another—rejoicing along with him. One finds this kind of love more usually in parents than in children. A father or mother will go to a lot of trouble to arrange a treat for a child, and feel amply rewarded in the pleasure the child gets out of it. Children can do the same thing for their parents, but do so less frequently.

On the supernatural level we can rejoice at the thought of how perfect God is, how wonderfully raised above all lack or limitation. We can so rejoice even when painfully conscious of our own needs. Have we not heard people in difficulties say quite sincerely "I'm glad that John is not here". In pain, in want, in doubt, we can be glad that God, Whom we love, is untouched by even the shadow of what we, as men, must endure. It is part of wisdom to think that nothing is too good for Our Father. Part of wisdom it also is to sing out loud in our hearts that nothing we may be destined to suffer is too much to pay for the glorious privilege of being and being called the sons of God Himself.

5

BEATIFIC VISION AND JOY

"LET us run by patience to the fight proposed to us; Looking on Jesus, the Author and Finisher of faith, who having joy set before him endured the cross, despising the shame, and now sitteth on the right hand of the throne of God".[1] The idea contained in this text is one which runs through St. Paul's epistles. The christian must keep heaven before his mind. In the hope of heaven he will find the joy and encouragement he needs to come triumphantly through the testing-time of life. Even apart from St. Paul's frequent mention of it, it is an idea which ought to suggest itself to any christian. For it is one of the most elementary of truths that we are not made for this world only: we are made for eternity and this world is but the way to eternity. The hope of seeing God at the end of our journey has been given us to lighten the weariness of the way.

One must admit, however, that most of us are slow to seek joy in the thought of heaven. Being body as well as soul, there is part of man which feels that here below is his rightful home and the world to come is exile. Faith tells us the opposite. But faith's voice is small and can scarce be heard above the insistent clamour of the body. We do not, of course, wish the voice of faith to sound in our ears unheeded. So, as often as not, we come to a working compromise. We try to belong to God in this world, try to find Him and love Him and serve Him in this world, and, for the

[1]Hebr. 12, 1-2.

rest, go on the assumption that this world is to last for ever. We want to be with God: but here, not in heaven. We want to continue with Him on the terms with which we are familiar. To see Him face to face strikes us rather as a plunge into the dark than as an entry into light. And implicit in it all is the soul's natural love for the body and its utter lack of experimental knowledge of how it could live without the body.

In vain do we counter these considerations—so many of them implicit and never to be expressed even to ourselves—with what we know by faith. Eternal glory remains vague and shadowy. We are ready to forgo it if only we may continue to hold what we now are. There is no gainsaying that Heaven, taken with all its implications of entry through the gateway of death, does not awaken immediate enthusiasm. We must accustom ourselves to the thought of it. We must pray for the desire and love of it. Only then will it become what it always ought to be, the light of the distant home, inspiring hope and awakening desire.

*   *   *   *

It is not easy when writing of heaven to do more than set down a very short series of unadorned statements. For heaven is a mystery and a most sublime one. The soul in beatitude enjoys the face to face vision of God, which is a sharing in God's own life. The mystery of the life of the soul in glory is part of that of the unsearchable glory of God Himself, "the King of Kings and the Lord of Lords; who only hath immortality and inhabiteth light inaccessible; whom no man hath seen or can see . . .".[2] Yet it is needful for us to think, however inadequately, about heaven. Otherwise our life is little more than pointless: "If in this life only we have hope in Christ we are of all men most miserable".[3] While admitting and believing firmly in the goodness of the world as it proceeds from the hand of God, the christian must also admit and believe firmly that he has not in the world a lasting city:

---

[2] I Tit. 6, 15-16.
[3] I Cor. 15, 19.

he is an exile living on earth a life without roots and devoting himself to preparing for the day when he can leave for home. This it is that makes his life pointless unless he integrates it firmly into the wholeness of eternal life. What fulness of joy can faith yield if it is not allowed to linger on the articles " . . . the resurrection of the body and life everlasting" ? What sort of hope has one if it looks to grace only and not beyond grace to glory? What kind of love of God is it that cherishes Him hidden behind the veil of faith, but is reluctant to meet Him in vision? Answering these questions we see how, apart from the future possession of heaven, the christian life is of all the most miserable. Not in the sense that the christian is doomed during his stay on earth to be more miserable than the *bon vivant*, and only the hope of heaven is there to make life tolerable, but in the sense that heaven is worked into the fabric of the christian life, and if, *per impossibile*, heaven were to be taken away from it, the whole fabric would be rent from top to bottom.

We read in the Second Book of Machabees how the seven young men encouraged themselves and were encouraged by their mother to suffer a most cruel death, by the thought that God Who had formed them and called them to mortal life could, after death, call them to eternal life. It is only natural thus to have recourse to the strengthening thought of heaven in time of trial. When suffering in mind or in body it is good to remember that we look to a life where suffering will cease and God will wipe all tears from our eyes. However severe it may be, the suffering of the moment is of a moment only, and if borne in love and patience it will contribute to meriting an eternity of joy. The problem of pain agitates many minds. In the last resort we need a practical rather than a theoretical solution to it, something to help us to accept it rather than something to explain how it fits into the scheme of things. A most practical solution is that there is nothing final about the pain of this world. We who suffer can look beyond our sufferings to a life in which it has no place. This, of course, is not the only practical solution to be found. Union of our suffering with the redemptive suffering of Jesus is another, and a most fruitful one. But it is important not to underestimate the value of the hope of heaven as a help to bearing the cross. It reveals suffering in its true dimensions by reminding us that it is for a time only, and reveals it in its possibilities of fruitfulness by reminding us that it can be meritorious of heaven. St. Thérèse of the Child Jesus, we are told, was helped considerably in her spiritual ascent by the thought of heaven and of the reward God had laid up there for her. There is nothing cowardly in turning from pain to the thought of eternal joy. It is simply one of the means given to human weakness by God to become strong in the time of trial. The hope of heaven is part of the armour of God which we pull on in time of battle so that we may play a christian's part—we who without it might have played a coward's.

*   *   *   *

Life in heaven consists essentially in seeing and loving God. That is the usual formula. A more attractive one would be that it is being in God's company, being admitted to the family circle of the Blessed Trinity. By combining the two formulas we can arrive at a better understanding of what they both express so inadequately: that life in heaven consists essentially in the knowledge and love of God within the intimacy of the Godhead.

First of all, it is important to banish from the ideas of knowing, seeing and loving as used in this context any suggestion whatever of being at a distance from God. Here on earth we may see a person who passes us at a distance and instinctively be well-disposed towards him, which means to love him. There is no question of so seeing and loving God in heaven. To find an analogy we must think rather of the seeing and knowing and loving of members of a family gathered together at home in the evening. Even when no word is spoken between them they are happy in one another's presence. And their happiness is of a kind which surpasses every other happiness natural to man. Friendship is the greatest of human experiences and the source of the most intense human joys. And among friendships that of family life—if friendship is not too weak a word to express the relationship of family oneness—is the highest. Friendship is man enjoying man, man in communion with the highest this world holds; and family friendship is the closest such communion. Seeing and knowing God must therefore be understood on the analogy of the family—in terms of immediate communion of man with God, of man who was made for God with God Who made man for Himself.

At a first glance there appears to be something static about seeing and knowing, and almost instinctively we reject it as a definition of friendship in favour of some more dynamic concept such as mutual communication or revealing of soul to soul. This is a point which could lead one far afield in discussing friendship. Certain aspects of the problem do not concern us vitally here, such as that all mutual communication must of necessity tend to a possessive repose of knowledge and love. Communication, as we experience it in human friendship, is but the beginning of a process which is fully achieved in mutual acceptance and possession: like every other movement, communication tends to a goal which is no longer movement but rest. And viewed from this angle it could be pointed out that our communion with God in heaven is one of possession: not that we grasp Him fully, but that He utters Himself to us without reserve.

The point on which I should, however, like to linger is this: that our communion with God in heaven is of a kind which contains within itself in a supereminent way all that makes the thrill of self-communication in friendship so heart-warming. Our seeing God is, in fact, God communicating Himself to us. To see God is to have the living Word of God uttered in the depths of one's soul. To rest lovingly in the vision of God is to hold this utterance in unending rapture. Every human word, however eloquent, dies out, its significance exhausted. Not so the Word of God. That Word alone is rich enough to be capable of unending utterance. The human analogy to the soul's possession of God in heaven is, therefore, something like this: a moment of intense communication in human friendship, drawn out unendingly in all its first freshness; a word charged with love, sustained undyingly. Whatever the philosopher may say, and however true what he says may be, there is something in the moments when friend struggles to reveal himself to friend, which seems lacking in the repose of established friendship. Somehow the soul reveals itself across the muddle of inadequate words in a way which we miss when the words have been spoken and friendship rests on their memory. Beatific vision is an ever-spoken word, a friendship always revealing itself, a friendship caught in the very moment of self-revelation and held there by the unfathomable richness of the Friend Who stands revealed.

*   *   *   *

Seeing God is therefore more than looking at Him. It is the knowledge of close friendship, that act of the mind—call it by whatever name you will—in which friend stands revealed to friend. It is worth while now to retrace our steps somewhat so as to arrive once more at this same conclusion, picking up, perhaps, a little extra understanding for our pains.

Some few months ago I visited Rome for the first time. Walking alone through its streets there was a lot I could recognize unaided. Memories of badly learned history and desultory studies in art awoke at unexpected moments peopling a heap of ruins with early martyrs or urging me in quest of a particular statue or painting in places where there seemed already more than enough to keep the sightseer busy. Had I known nothing of Rome's christian and cultural past I should have seen much but grasped little in my solitary walks. As it was, I could feel somewhat at home, even though conscious that there was much that I must have missed.

On one occasion I had the happiness of going out with a friend who knew Rome well. His help made a world of difference to my sight-seeing. He drew attention to this or that monument, or filled in, in a few pregnant sentences, a historical background. Relying no longer on my own powers of perception, aided by a certain amount of general culture, Rome began to live for me. I became in some way coeval with Rome, knowing her through the centuries and seeing her now in the light of her richly varied life. All that was mine as the result of a friend's words. How much more Rome would have meant to me if it had been possible to see through his very eyes, to know Rome with his mind rather than with my own and to love her with his affection.

Being in God's presence, seeing and knowing Him in Heaven, is not a matter of admiring Him from outside and being enraptured by what one can grasp of Him. It is not even a matter of meeting Him in the company of Jesus and Mary and learning from their lips—those human lips of Theirs whose utterances we shall hear in Heaven—all He has done for us and for souls, all He is in Himself. True, Jesus and Mary will allow us to enter in some way into Their intimacy with the Trinity. But that is not the essence of beatific vision. Its essence is to see God by entering into His own knowing of Himself.[4] To know God in heaven is to embrace, though not to exhaust, His own knowledge of Himself: to love Him is to thrill to His own love of Himself. Friends wish to reveal themselves fully to their friends. They can never do so. Words and actions, by which alone they can communicate, are not themselves, are but representations or hints of what they truly are. God alone can communicate intimacy with Himself by Himself entering into the very mind. Similarly with love. The human friend on earth is drawn to his friend by the magnetism of personality revealing itself through various contacts and encounters. In heaven God enters our will and becomes the weight which draws us to Himself. In

<hr>

[4]Scholastic theology teaches that in the Beatific Vision the Divine Essence takes the place of created species in the act of knowing. Something analogous happens in the act of loving. There is no point in discussing this very technical matter here. It is mentioned merely to show how the Divine Essence enters into the very act whereby we know and love God beatifically.

both knowing and loving Him, there is complete immediacy. We see the very Truth and Beauty He sees: we embrace Him in the very clasp in which Father, Son and Holy Ghost are eternally united. The life of heaven is, in the fullest sense, a share in the life of God. Not simply in that it is a life closely resembling His, but in that we are introduced into the very knowing and loving in which His life consists.

*   *   *   *

Though the Divine Essence is laid bare to the soul in the beatific vision, in no sense does the soul know or love God as fully as He does Himself. God alone is capable of knowing and loving Himself adequately. The soul knows and loves Him only in the measure of its capacity. But this does not in any way take from the immediacy of its vision and love. Somewhat, perhaps, as the selfsame ocean which is contained fully only within its bed, is yet present in a partial way in every creek and bay and inlet, so God, grasped fully by Himself only is partially present to every soul. And yet, this image is—as in such a matter all images must be—as much misleading as helpful. For though the ocean itself is present in the creek or bay, yet not all the ocean is there, whereas the full Divinity is present to the beatified soul. In heaven the soul has an inadequate grasp of the whole of the Divine Essence, not a full grasp of only part (The Divine Essence, in any case, cannot be divided into parts). And in this context the term "inadequate" means merely "not fully exhaustive". For judged in relation to the capacity of the soul, its knowledge of God is anything but inadequate: rather does it measure up to the full limit of its actual power to know.

Thus, the soul in heaven sees God Himself, but does not and could not exhaust fully the rich infinity of God's know-ableness. Therein lies one of the reasons why the life of Beatific Vision, in spite of its changelessness, is so fully satisfying. It is a life in which mind and will have reached their final term, an Object seen and loved not in words, images and the like, but in Its very Self; an Object, which, even when grasped, melts as it were into glorious horizons, leaving the soul enraptured both with what it can see and with what it knows is beyond its full comprehension. The vision of God is the complete fulfilment of the soul's desire. There are moments on earth—for example, when in the course of a walk one reaches a point whence opens a view of lake, or sea or mountain majesty—and one says: "There is no need to go any further. Here we have just what we want." There is no need, no possibility of going further than the vision of God. In it the soul has all and more than it could want, and its quest for peace in fulness of life and experience has come to a close.

Face to face with God and seeing Him, as it were, through His own eyes, the soul enjoys ecstatic contemplation of the deep mysteries of the Godhead: how God is Three in One; sees the Word proceeding from and yet united in oneness of Nature with the Father; sees the Holy Ghost, the Personal bond of love of Father and Son, proceeding from Both, yet remaining one with Them in all except Personality. Besides these mysteries of the Triune God, the soul contemplates the Divine Nature: Its Infinite Perfection, Its Immensity, Its Eternity and all those other attributes of which theology can tell us now only enough to whet our desire for fuller knowledge. All this the soul knows in proportion to its capacity. No aspect of the Godhead is hidden from it. The only limitation there is arises from its inability to enclose God within the limited scope of its mind, elevated though this is by the light of glory.

But whereas all of God is open to the soul's gaze, not all that He has done in creation need be so revealed. Though this is a matter about which there is not full theological certainty, it is commonly held that the soul in glory will see in God those of His works with which she is in any way concerned. One of God's works which we shall see however in full detail in Him is man. No man is alien to us. All men are called to the one vocation in Christ Jesus. It is becoming therefore that God should keep no secrets from us in regard to our fellow-men. But matters which do not touch us, and in which, in any case, our happiness does not consist nor can they add to it, may well be a secret from us for all eternity.

The fact that the soul may know in God that certain of its relatives have been lost eternally in no way diminishes beatific peace and joy. God is more a Father to man than we are to our children. If He can condemn certain of His children to hell for all eternity it must be for a reason which accords fully with His Love and Mercy and His Eternal Peace. What that reason is we are incapable of grasping completely now. But in heaven we shall know Hell's place in His eternal designs, and being like Him, our peace and joy will remain full, even as His unchangeably is.

*　　　　*　　　　*　　　　*

In spite of all that revelation tells us about heaven and the prodigality with which image has been heaped on image to make it take body in our minds, it remains true that the essential and spiritual side of beatitude eludes our understanding. It is too near to the mystery of the life of God Himself to be capable of full expression in terms familiar to a created mind. Hence the value of the accidental and bodily side of beatitude which is so much more easily grasped and which, apart from its own attractiveness, is richly suggestive of the spiritual glory of which it is but the setting.

It is a dogma of faith that, on the Last Day, the body will rise again, to share with the soul its reward or punishment. We are concerned here only with the resurrection of the bodies of the just.

Soul and body—the same body which partnered the soul in mortal life—enter into the joy of eternity. But each does so in its own way. As God is purely spiritual, His union with the mind and will are immediate, and without intervening sensation. On earth, of course, nothing is known except through or to the accompaniment of the senses' activity. This does not however mean that the body united to the soul in glory has no share in the soul's life. To begin with, there will be a certain overflowing of joy from soul to body. For body and soul make up one person and the beatific joy of the soul will—as even intellectual joys do on earth—make itself felt in the body which is so closely united with it.

But that is not all. The senses of the glorified body will have objects on which to exercise themselves and from this exercise will take rise a new accidental joy distinct from that of essential beatitude. With our eyes we shall see Jesus and Mary and Joseph and the whole court of the just. To see Jesus or Mary—would that not be happiness enough for a man's eternity? We shall hear the words they utter and with our own lips speak to them. Like the beloved disciple, we shall draw near to Jesus and touch Him with reverent love and feel the warmth of His saving embrace as He welcomes us and wipes from our eyes the tears of a lifetime. Our bodies will be all glorious: free from blemish, free from defect and raised above the usual earthly limitations in the matter of movement from place to place. What a thrilling experience it will be to move among the ranks of the blessed and, the soul still filled with the enrapturing vision of God, pass from one of His servants to another, seeing at every step how wonderful God is in His saints! Shall we ever reach the end of the ranks of the blessed? Shall we linger on, perhaps, near the Sacred Humanity and the Queen of Heaven, content to know that we are in the company of a countless multitude any one of whom is a friend to bring joy to a human heart? Whatever we do, this accidental bliss of ours will never pall. Jesus and Mary make an eternal appeal to man: the countless throng of the blessed are an almost unlimited possibility of friendship in comparison with which those of earth are but empty and deceptive shadows.

The dogma of the resurrection of the body was dear to the early martyrs. They offered their body to the torturer and to wild beasts strong in the faith that on the last day they would receive it back glorified from God. Perhaps it is to our loss that we think less of the body now when the thought of heaven is before our minds. God Who has made us soul and body means us to tend to Him soul and body and attain to

Him, soul and body. At least during certain periods of their lives, all will find light and encouragement in considering the part reserved to the body in eternal beatitude. There is the participated glorification of their own bodies to look forward to; and still more, the special happiness which will be theirs through the bodily vision of the Sacred Humanity of Jesus and the incarnate motherliness of Mary. In heaven, of course, God will be all in all: in Him will our boundless joy consist. But it is no negligible thing that that joy will be ours in the company of Jesus and Mary. They who light our way through life will themselves shine resplendent on our eyes in the light of eternity.

*   *   *   *

This is perhaps the moment to return to a point treated briefly in an earlier chapter—that of the beatific vision in Jesus during His life on earth. We have seen the theological reasons which explain the appropriateness of His Sacred Humanity being so endowed, all of which reduce themselves in the last analysis to the unique union in Him of the Human and the Divine. It remains merely to glance at some of the ways in which the Beatific Vision was worked into the pattern of His mortal life.

Jesus was both *viator* and *comprehensor,* One walking the road of human existence and One in the full and joyous consciousness of having reached its end. His mind was open both to the events of daily life and to the full splendour of the Divine Essence. His will was fixed in joyous love on the performance of His Father's Will within His human setting of time and place; and, simultaneously, was lost in ecstatic love of the Father Himself, One and Unchanging throughout eternity. In His life of feeling and emotion Jesus remained *viator* and *comprehensor.* On the one hand, His Humanity, being truly human and retaining its human affective capacities, reacted in a human way to the experiences It underwent. Physical objects could cause Him pleasure and pain. Their memory could do the same, as also the anticipation of what was about to happen. This normal function-

ing of the affective life—and it is of special importance to
note it in regard to pain—was not hampered by the fact that
the same Sacred Humanity, the same soul of Jesus, was, at a
higher level inundated with the joy of face to face possession
of the Godhead. This took place through a special dispen-
sation. St. Thomas tells us that the effects of the beatific
vision in Jesus' soul were in some way held in check so as
not to render suffering impossible.[5] This does not mean that
the joy of the Beatific vision exercised no influence whatever
on Jesus' sufferings. He Who suffered and He Who joyed
was one Person, suffering and joying in the one human nature.
It was with a will transformed by beatific joy that Jesus bore
suffering. What we must insist on is that His suffering was
real, not that His joy contributed in no way to His bearing it.
Even in our own lives joy and suffering can co-exist, and joy
strengthens the will to endure what it naturally shrinks from.
Jesus, we may say, extracted the last ounce of goodness out
of suffering. For He saw it in the Father's eternal designs, saw
its full worth, saw how to make it the occasion of the greatest
good. And then with a heart wholly absorbed in His Father,
He accepted suffering as it fell under His permissive will.
Jesus and Jesus alone was in the position of seeing life in
the full light of eternity and learning in that light that God's
Will is our peace and joy.[6] We, whose lives are a sharing in
His, see this in the dim light of faith. Yet even that light is
sufficient to enkindle within us something of the loving and

---

[5] IIIa, Q 46, a8.

[6] The idea of accepting suffering is not entirely free from ambiguity.
Jesus accepted His Cross in itself as the altar upon which the sacrifice
of Calvary would be offered. Others of His sufferings—those of a
kind which when they enter into our lives we term our crosses—He
accepted in a different way. Take, for example, the tiredness He
experienced as He rested by Jacob's well. That He accepted and
offered to His Father by not allowing it to restrain Him from working for the salvation of the soul of the Samaritan woman: He
accepted it, in other words, not in itself but as part of the milieu in
which He was to work for His Father's glory and the salvation of
souls. This is the way in which we also must normally accept our
crosses: we bear them in an act which is incidental to our direct
interest, which is the love of God and our fellowmen.

joyous acceptance of the whole of God's Will which, in its perfection was Jesus' and His alone.

The cry of Jesus on the Cross, "My God, My God why hast thou forsaken me?" preserved for us in the Gospel of St. Matthew[7] creates sometimes a difficulty about admitting that He experienced beatific joy on the Cross itself. There at least, we feel, and in however small a measure, was joy diminished and darkness spread across the face of Jesus' soul. A suggestion of the kind is sometime met in spiritual authors, as if on the Cross the beatific vision was in some mysterious way obscured.

Theologically there is no foundation for making any such exception to the general rule of Jesus' face to face communion with and joy in His Father. St. Thomas treats the problem in his commentary on the text quoted [8] and explains it with his usual lucidity. Jesus was abandoned by His Father only in the sense that His Father allowed the Jews and the Roman soldiery to work their wills unhindered on Him. In this sense, a person is said to be abandoned if he does not receive the help to which he might appear to be entitled. Thus the Father withdrew from Jesus not the comforting vision of His Face but the protection of His hand.

*   *   *   *

Speaking of the vision he had of heaven's bliss St. Paul said "I know such a man (whether in the body or out of the body I know not: God knoweth); that he was caught up into paradise and heard secret words which it is not granted to man to utter".[9] Theologians dispute whether in this experience St. Paul was granted a passing experience of the beatific vision. Whatever be the nature of the rapture of which he speaks his concluding words are applicable to our problem—" . . . heard secret words which it is not given to man to utter". Heaven, and even the approaches to heaven (if, in fact, it is not of the

---

[7]Mt. 27, 46.
[8]In Evangelium S. Matthaei Commentaria.
[9]2 Cor. 12, 3-4.

beatific vision that he speaks) are so far above human experience, aided though it be by faith and the gifts of the Holy
Ghost, that when all has been said one must recognize that
the ultimate tribute to be paid to it is one of humble silence.
How much there is in God's presence as experienced in prayer
which we can never adequately express in words. What then
of His presence as experienced in beatific love and vision.
"Eye hath not seen, nor ear heard, neither hath it entered into
the heart of man, what things God hath prepared for them
that love Him".[10] In one word only can the beatific vision be
expressed, in the Uncreated Word uttered eternally by the
Father.

---

[10] I Cor. 2, 9.

6

GROWTH IN JOY

THE fact that there is such a thing as growth in peace or joy is frequently brought home to us in the lives of the saints. Their last years on earth are usually characterized by a serenity and by a radiant joyousness which astonishes those who knew them in their earlier years, marked though these were by a more than common spirit of deep contentment. One finds something similar in the life of Jesus. The sustained outpouring of joy we meet in St. John's account of the Last Supper has no parallel elsewhere in the pages of the Gospel. A moment which one might have thought should lie completely under the shadow of Calvary, proves to have been one eagerly awaited and relished to the full. On no other occasion does Jesus so pour Himself out in gladness into the souls of his Apostles. He is glad that His work has been accomplished, glad that His hour has come, glad that He is to rejoin the Father—so many gladnesses which were not His before, and which find their echo in the gladness of the saint who has fought the good fight and looks to the just and merciful Judge for a crown of glory.

Joy never so grows on earth as to be completely full. Jesus spoke of the blessedness of the poor in spirit, of the meek, of those that hunger and thirst after justice . . . of the christian, in short. But, though truly blessed, the christian cannot in this world be completely blessed. The beatitude or happiness which is his is that known to theologians as imperfect. There is always in it some admixture of pain, or at least—and this is itself a form of pain—some sense of incompleteness. But though imperfect it is not static. The christian life on earth is one of progressive approach to that of heaven. Not that the happiness of the christian will normally reach such a pitch towards the end of his days here below that heaven will be nothing more than a single step forward in the same direction: vision is not just something more than faith, it is something on a higher level. Neither is it true that the joy of one's later years will of necessity be less broken by trials, even interior ones, than those of first conversion: the cross remains the christian's lot all the days, however long, of his pilgrimage in time. His growth in joy will be such as to allow of bearing, if it be God's will, a greater burden of pain. But his joy will be such as to make the burden light and even when he groans in the agony of one crushed, within the depths of his soul there will be peace, as it were a voice of joyous singing, which will be a true foretaste of eternal bliss.

*   *   *   *

Speaking in very general terms, we may distinguish two kinds of joy, acquired and infused: the one resulting more immediately from our efforts, the other poured into the soul by God. More correctly we ought to speak of two sources of joy, our grace-aided efforts and God's goodness. For, ultimately, all spiritual joy is caused by grace. But as sometimes our action and sometimes God's is more evident in our growth in joy, the division into acquired and infused may be adopted in practice. Here we are concerned with joy in the normal christian life and omit all consideration of exceptional graces which may or may not be given according to God's good pleasure.

At the very outset, and before considering acquired joy, it is important to note that there is an element of infused joy even in an undeveloped christian life. In fact, there is a rich latent source of joy in such a life, awaiting the liberating influence of union with God and detachment from the world in order to make its presence noticed. Provided he is in the state of grace, the christian has the infused virtues—among which faith, hope and charity are included—and the gifts of the Holy Ghost. Through these he has a vision of God and life and an attitude to God and life which, however imperfectly, bring peace and joy to his soul. To the extent, however slight, to which his life is influenced by faith, hope and charity and, among the gifts, by wisdom especially, there is a feeling of sureness about it which is God's gift to him by grace. He may, unfortunately, advert to this too infrequently, due to his main interests being other than those connected with the life of grace.

This consideration suggests at once the first element in the acquisition of spiritual joy: detachment from all that is alien to it. Traditionally this is summed up as detachment from the three great concupiscences, that of the eyes, that of the flesh and that known as the pride of life. And among the many aspects under which these three concupiscences may be considered the one which seems most relevant to the point under discussion just now is their common tendency to introduce pain and to dry up the sources of true joy.

God made man soul and body and placed him in the setting of a material world. His happiness is conditioned by his attitude to the relationships so set up by God. If he holds soul and body and uses the world in harmony with God's designs, grace can flower as happiness within him. If on the contrary, his attitude to soul or body or the world sets him at variance with God—and consequently with his true self—an element of chaos and disorder is introduced which makes happiness impossible.

The concupiscence of the eyes concerns a man's attitude to the world, more especially to its material wealth. The world and all that is in it was made by God for man's use. Hence there is a form of possession and use of the world which in no way conflicts with happiness. It consists in possessing and using the world in submission to God's will and in full recognition that a man is never more than a steward of what he is said to possess and must at all times be ready to relinquish his stewardship and render an account of it. So held and used, the wealth of this world becomes an instrument of good. It is subordinated to grace, and by becoming the object or the means to virtuous action serves often as the occasion of the experience of christian joy. Thus, the material world and its wealth are not of themselves hostile to joy. That they become only when they are the object of an inordinate attachment. Used, say, for the support and education of one's family, for providing more christian forms of employment, for the relief of the poor, for the spread of the Church's activity in mission lands, money has a rightful place in the christian life and contributes to bringing God's peace and joy on earth.

Money becomes an obstacles to joy when a man seeks it for its own sake or uses it for unworthy purposes. It does this, in the first place, by stifling the life of grace in his soul or by killing it altogether if his attitude to it is gravely sinful. By making money an end in itself a man withdraws his life from God completely or in part. Grace means little to him. He does not make generous use of faith, hope and charity and the other typically christian virtues. The result is that the flow of joy from God to him is blocked. The channels by which grace and peace might flow into his soul—his mind, his will and all his other powers—carry a full load of interest in and care about money, and the supernatural can find little room to pass along them. And this happens even when he has not fully abandoned the principles of christianity. For once money has become a genuine end, christianity is relegated to the place of a part-time interest. Its spiritual richness is, of necessity, poorly appreciated and it ceases to be reckoned as that which alone gives meaning and relish to life.

An inordinate attachment to money stifles true joy in another way also. The possession of money—and even the intense desire to possess it—causes a type of exhilaration and enthusiasm which deludes the soul into believing that it has found a way of life that has something worth-while to offer. There is joy and joy, true joy and false joy. And false joy is like enough to true joy to create the illusion that it is satisfying. That is one of the reasons why the non-christian is so little impressed by what we tell him of christian joy. He has a joy of his own. It gives him satisfaction. He can with difficulty conceive of joy of any other type. Most particularly does he find it hard to conceive of a joy which does not arise from contacts with what one can see and hear and touch. With his senses as the test of the real and immediate gain as the final criterion of value, christianity seems to offer him but a mere illusion—a pleasing one perhaps, and even a noble one, but none the less an illusion. And this is true, in due proportion, of the christian who lives most of his life at the same level of appreciation of values. This world gives him so much satisfaction, and his faith, as he practises it, so very little, that he finds no reason to believe that a more christian life would be for him a more satisfying one: "And others fell among thorns, and the thorns grew up and choked them."[1]

A third injury which attachment to money may do to the soul is that it creates inner and outer conflicts. Inner conflicts: those between the claims of God's law and the desire of possessing; those between the invitations to a more deeply christian life which come to everybody, and the urge to leave even more time and energy for material advancement. Outer conflicts: conflicts within the family who may feel neglected, or may clamour for more than they have; conflicts with an apparently wasteful wife and

---

[1] Mt. 13, 7.

extravagant children; conflicts with business rivals; envy
of others' more rapid promotion. All these are so many
experiences which shatter the fabric of spiritual joy and
make life a long torture.

It would, of course, be naive even to suggest that an
inordinate attachment to money is found only in those
who aim resolutely at being rich. Even the poor can be
inordinately attached to money—to the money they wish
to have, to the money others have and which they envy,
to the money that would raise them from the want against
which they rebel. Today there is so much that money can
provide, such a variety of luxuries and gadgets, that it is
hard for a christian no matter what his income to escape
the desire to have more than he can, let alone to leave what
he has in God's hands. St. Paul's words are as true today
as when he first wrote them: "For the desire of money is
the root of all evils: which some coveting have erred from
the faith, and have entangled themselves in many sorrows."[2]

*   *   *   *

The evils which result from an inordinate attachment to
the flesh and from self-will are so like those which result
from an inordinate attachment to money that it would be
pointless to go through them in detail. Worth noting, however, is the fact that sins of the flesh would seem to be
opposed to christian joy principally in that they offer a
spurious substitute while at the same time so coarsening
the soul that it can with difficulty appreciate the spiritual.
Sins of self-will such as the inordinate desire for complete
self-determination would, on the other hand, seem to be
opposed to christian joy rather through the inner and outer
conflicts—leading as they well may to utter frustration—
which they occasion. The man who wills and wills fiercely
to be the sole master of his life is racked both by the sense
of his inability to give effect to his desire and by the un-
wanted factors which crowd into his life and refuse to fit

---

[2] I Tim. 6, 10.

into his scheme of things. It will, therefore, be more profitable to mention briefly the good use that may be made of the flesh and the will, so that they may be allowed to contribute their full quota to the total of christian joy.

God has given us flesh and blood that through flesh and blood we may find Him and our neighbour. Husband, wife and children are held together in the family by ties of flesh and blood that they may help one another to know and love God, and learn from their intimacy with one another the beauty and worth of all that is clothed in human flesh and blood. The family is a school in the art of giving. This is another way of saying that it is a school in the art of love of God and man. Which, in its turn, is another way of saying that it is a school of joy. There is joy in giving, joy in being charitable, joy in loving. There is joy too in receiving when one receives in love from one who is loved. The flesh opens all this up to us. We abuse it only when we linger over it, neglecting to go beyond its attraction to the love of God and man. What a wonderful, and what a wonderfully joyous saint he is, who brings to his love of God and man the essence of the affection which he bears to the members of his family!

The free will, too, has a positive part to play in the christian life. It has been given man by God that he may use it to choose freely the end or purpose to which he will direct his life and the means he considers suitable to attain it. He abuses it if he deliberately makes choice of the wrong end or if he adopts means which offend God, and which, in consequence, cannot lead to his true end. Man is truly the master of his life, even if the exercise of this capacity depends on God. And being free he can enjoy, however humbly, a sense of self-determination in all he does and all he plans to do.

Hence freedom of choice is at once a source and condition of human joy: a source, in that it empowers a man to choose from among the various ways of life in which joy is found; a condition, in that joy springs from the activity of the will which is ever deepening its attachment to its true purpose and applying itself vigorously to the use of well-adapted means. This is, of course, to be understood in no narrowly selfish sense. The end of human life is not God possessed by the individual for himself alone, but God possessed by him in the great family group of the angels and saints drawn into the circle of the Father, Son and Holy Ghost through Jesus. In other words, it is God's glory, God glorified in me and in His angels and saints. The means adopted by the free will tend, in consequence, not only to my own sanctification, but also to the sanctification of all men through membership of the Church, Christ's Mystical Body. It is therefore right and proper—more than that, it is a glorious thing—to use the will freely for the Church. Which means using it not only in matters which concern immediately faith and morals, liturgy and personal devotion, but in all that limitless field of secular affairs where there are things to be ordered in accordance with the Church's teaching, and trends to be fostered which draw souls nearer to the Church.

The christian life allows, therefore, for the type of man who glories in the free exercise of his initiative in the service of the Church. Such a man will of necessity be guided by authority. But within the framework of authority —and it is a surprisingly loose one—he will spend his will in devising ways and means, testing new approaches and further exploring old ones. By approving the vow of obedience the Church does not mean to canonize the non-religious who does nothing except in response to a command. If obedience is best, freedom of initiative is good. The very obedience of the religious is the object of his free choice and he is expected, in his life and work, to use his initiative in regard to details of time and manner and method. It must always be borne in mind that a free, enterprising, initiative-loving will is a good thing: that is a

good and a satisfying thing to use it for God: that to lack
it or to allow it to rust is to miss much of what is worth-
while in human life. It would take us too far afield to
examine the different virtues of humility, prudence, courage
and all the rest which the man of initiative needs. But
granted his understanding of the Church's role in the world,
and granted his sincere desire to explore to the full what
he personally, and only he, can do, his freedom is a rich
mine of possibilities of living to the full. Far from fearing
it, he should thank God for it. Far from holding it in
constant check he should regard its non-use as sheer waste.

*   *   *   *

On the negative side, therefore, growth in joy may be
said to depend on self-denial. And, though we have considered it only with special reference to the three concupiscences, in fact it depends on self-denial in all its wide
sweep, for any form of self-indulgence or immortification
tends to choke it.

Turning now to the positive aids to growth in joy, it is
well to begin with a warning. Do not make joy—even
spiritual joy—the direct, much less the main, goal of your
life. In its essence joy is something incidental. It is the
accompaniment of harmonious life and action. Our purpose
must always be to do what is good and right, to love God
and our neighbour, to contribute in some way by our
actions to the glory of God and the salvation of souls,
among which our own soul is included. Doing such things
will make us joyous, provided the necessary conditions are
realized. But to aim at joy directly makes us selfish and
self-indulgent, and is, in fact, an expression of a selfish
and self-indulgent tendency. Far from succeeding, it defeats
its own purpose by reducing the number and intensity of
the acts from which joy would follow and by blocking
that flow of grace to the soul which is joy's ultimate source.

Granted all this, it remains true that there is a great deal we can do in a positive way—that is, over and above the removing of obstacles—to bring more joy into our christian lives.

In the first place we can pray for joy. Joy is something for which people ought to pray. Normally speaking—in other words, apart from times and stages of special trial— a christian's life ought to be joyous. If it is not joyous, the evil does not end with the lack of joy. Lack of joy can induce a still greater evil, lack of generosity. It is very difficult, without more than ordinary grace, to be really generous with God if the general tenor of one's life is joyless and spiritually bleak. I am not speaking now of the possibility of making a great act of generosity in a moment of deep interior desolation. Generous souls are called to make such acts. I am speaking rather of the general attitude towards God which will be adopted by a soul of average grace, if joy in God, joy in Christ, joy in christianity, is habitually lacking. Normally it will be one of fidelity to strict duty without anything of the keenly perceptive generosity of the joyous soul. "God loveth a cheerful giver,"[3] for the cheerful giver gives more of himself in his giving, and, incidentally, gives more in actual service. To pray for joy is, therefore, another way of praying for generosity. God may be withholding the grace of joy just in order to stimulate us to ask ourselves what are the implications of praying for it. He certainly does not wish us to settle down to being without it. And even if, for His own wise and loving reasons, He delays to answer our prayers fully, He will not delay to grant generosity which is, itself, a joy of a delicately spiritual kind that comes from giving with open hands.

*　　　*　　　*　　　*

It is remarkable how frequently St. Paul associates joy with the virtue of hope. It suggests that if we make, with

---

[3] 2 Cor. 9, 7.

the help of God's grace, more frequent and more generous use of the virtue of hope we are adopting one of the most effective means to grow in joy.

By hope we rely on God's power and grace to bring us through this world right up to the possession of Himself in beatific vision. It will contribute to our joy and our growth in joy in two ways. The first of these is by keeping us in mind that we are destined for unending and supreme happiness. The sufferings of this world, even the worst we may be called to endure, are not comparable with the total amount of joy which will be in our lives. We are like people walking home on a cold night along a muddy road who take neither cold nor mud too seriously because it will all be forgotten as soon as they are within doors. And if the road does happen to be long, they keep their spirits up by thinking of what awaits them at the end. It would be foolish to attempt to face the trials, or even the labours, of life with nothing more to ease them than the spiritual consolations and graces of the moment. Heaven, and the assurance that with God's help it is within our power to attain to, is the main source of christian courage and joy. Heaven is, in fact, the main part of our life, the eternal part. The part we live through on earth is short in itself and incredibly short in comparison with what is to follow.

Hope contributes to joy and growth in joy in a second way by reminding us that our trust is in God Himself: "Our help is in the name of the Lord Who made heaven and earth."[4] No one, relying on himself alone, can face the whole of life confidently. There are very definite limits also to what friends can do to help. But hope gives us God's Omnipotence as our support. And it is up to us to keep that in mind especially in times of trial and spiritual difficulties. There are different ways in which this habitual reliance on God and confidence in Him may be encouraged. One way is to form the habit of committing oneself

---

[4] Ps. 123, 8.

frequently to Jesus, our Saviour, the Source of all grace. Another is to strengthen one's conviction in Mary's Motherhood of men and of each man in particular. None of these methods is exclusive of the others and in effect they all amount to forming the firm conviction that God loves us and has placed His Infinite Power at our disposal. With such a conviction life can become joyous. Uncertainty, insecurity, fear of one's ability to meet the future—all these make deep and lasting joy impossible. Hope or confidence is, as it were, the foundation on which joy is built. Trusting in God we can face life joyously.

* * * *

It is a matter of common experience that the amount of joy a person finds in life depends not so much on the experience of the moment as on his habitual outlook. A person of an habitually gloomy outlook gets little and troubled pleasure from an evening's entertainment, whereas a mere nothing suffices to make a cheerful person more cheerful still. This is a fact to be borne in mind in regard to the spiritual life. In order to be joyous we must make the attempt to cultivate a joyous outlook, that is to say, we must recall frequently to mind those truths of faith which are joyous and inspiring. One time during which to recall them is that of mental prayer. Let our prayer be full of the thought of the great glory and happiness of the Blessed Trinity with Whom we shall be for all eternity; Jesus' triumph over sin and death and His glorious Ascension into heaven; Mary's loving power as Queen and Mother; the marvels grace has worked in our souls, such as Inhabitation and our incorporation into the Mystical Body; the sublime perfection of the virtues with which God has endowed us, especially faith, hope and charity; the invincible power of the Church and the merciful machinery of salvation committed to it. Such thoughts tend to inflame the will. And then we thank God for His great glory, rejoice in Jesus' triumph, pray to Mary that we may realize how true her motherhood is, affirm our loyalty to the Church and our conviction that she is God's bountiful and indestructible way of salvation. Other themes, such as those of sorrow for sin and our utter nothingness apart from God, will, of course, find their due place in our mental prayer. The point being made now is simply that we must not neglect the themes that lift up our hearts. Prayer is intended to be a source of joy and courage not only through the grace it wins for us but also through the state of mind which is developed through the vision it opens up of all that is consoling and glorious and triumphant in our faith.

What is true of mental prayer is true also of the ejaculations which we utter in the course of the day. At the beginning of our spiritual life ejaculations help to establish an habitual outlook: later on they are the expression of an established outlook. It is a mistake to select our ejaculations exclusively from among such as " God, be merciful to me a sinner", "Jesus, mercy: Mary, help", just as it would be a mistake, and a very serious one to make no use of those which remind us of our weakness and of our need of grace. In order that joy may find its rightful place in life we ought to include among our ejaculations some such as "Sacred Heart of Jesus, I place my trust in Thee", saying it not in a semi-despairing way but with the full assurance that trust placed in Jesus is not misplaced. Other similar ejaculations which suggest themselves are: "My soul doth magnify the Lord", "He that is mighty hath done great things", "Give praise to the Lord for He is good", Into Thy hands, O Lord, I commend my spirit", "Praise the Lord, all ye nations", "Jesus, Mary and Joseph, I give you my heart and soul." As has been mentioned, it is important that these and similar ejaculations when made issue from a glad heart, or a heart that realizes that it has more than reason enough to be glad—which amounts to the same thing. The mere mechanical repetition of the formulae produces little effect—though it does produce some effect.

What is of most value is to put our heart into them, or, when we cannot do that, to wish to put our heart into them.

These recommendations about subjects for mental prayer and the kind of ejaculations to make in the course of the day may at a first glance seem to be nothing more than a naturalistic auto-suggestion technique. That of course would not be sufficient to condemn them. It is right and necessary to make use of the findings of modern psychology in shaping our minds and wills to Jesus' image. But there is more than that in them. They are part of the way in which we are asked by God to co-operate with the grace He has poured into our souls. His grace is one which finds expression in joy and glad thanksgiving and hope no less than in sorrow for sin and humility. More particularly at the beginning of the spiritual life, and even at a later stage if one has neglected to do so already, the soul must co-operate consciously with grace in so expressing itself. To select God's great glory as a subject of mental prayer is therefore, not to force oneself into an artifically induced attitude of blissful adoration. On the contrary it amounts quite simply to placing the soul in circumstances in which its infused capacity for blissful adoration will find easy or spontaneous expression. Let us be quite clear that God has poured joy and triumph and hope and all the rest into our hearts. If we do not find them filling our lives with their splendid energies, it may be because we do not provide the appropriate outlet for them. They are, perhaps sealed up within us and we foolishly wonder why the little of grace to which we do allow expression fails to bring about the Thabor transformation which we believed was promised in every christian vocation.

*   *   *   *

Ultimately our growth in joy will be measured by our intimacy with God: Father, Son and Holy Ghost. First of all, because from God comes all grace, which is the root of joy implanted in the soul. Secondly, because actual joy arises chiefly from knowing and loving God, that is to say, from being intimate with Him and bound to Him. One way of increasing, with the help of grace, our intimacy with the Three Divine Persons is to turn to them frequently during mental prayer. Presupposing the act of faith by which we believe in Them and know Them, this is done principally by adoration and love. It is not at all necessary, nor is it even possible—since Their Mystery is the highest and the most removed from any created understanding—to have any great wealth of conceptual knowledge of Them in Their inner personal being. Much of what we know of the Divine Persons considered separately is predicated of Them only by way of appropriation and is actually true of all Three. That is the way in which we know the Father as Creator, the Son as God's enlightening Truth and the Holy Ghost as God's overflowing Love. And though appropriation does give a certain inadequate understanding of the Divine Persons in Themselves, it does so only by, as it were, apportioning among Them those characteristics which are common to all Three. Theology tells us a little more about that which makes each Divine Person to be Himself. But even the most learned theologian of the Trinity realizes that he is dealing with a mystery and that the concepts he makes use of, though valid and meaningful, always halt far short of vision. Even when elaborated into theology, faith has but little to say of the Blessed Trinity. That little is, however, unendingly rich in suggestiveness: not in the suggestiveness which leads primarily to further knowledge, but in that deeper suggestiveness which leads to adoringly admiring contemplation.

That is why adoration counts so much in our living contact with the Blessed Trinity. Three Infinite and Equal Persons in One Infinite God; the Father eternally generating the Son, His complete expression; The Holy Ghost proceeding from Father and Son by way of Their boundless mutual love . . . We adore Thee, Father, Son and Holy Ghost.

Our minds falter; our wills are more adapted than are our lips to express Who You are and who we are.

Such adoration is joy and spiritual exultation. Adoring God is a way of recognizing the beauty of the universe: that above and beyond all pain, disorder and misery there are the Three in Whom is peace—our peace and the peace of the world: in Whom is order and in Whom order will be restored: in Whom is beatitude and to Whose beatitude men are called. To adore is more than to admit we are nothing: it is to direct ourselves to the All, the Fulness that knows no lack. Insensibly adoration is charged with love. We who are nothing give ourselves, and the All is given in return. Beginning with the time of mental prayer, adoration and love of the Trinity diffuse themselves throughout our day, we co-operating by the deliberate use of ejaculations, moments of recollection and the like.

At this point it is necessary for us to be on our guard against any narrow formalism in our understanding of the pre-eminent importance of union with the Father and the Son and the Holy Ghost. It does not mean that we must aim at all times in making the Blessed Trinity the object of our prayer and in regarding Them as the only source of all our good and the goal of all our activity. It is a matter of sacred history that they did not give Themselves immediately to man. They gave Themselves to man in Jesus, that is to say, in the Man Who was also God. Through Him we have access to the Blessed Trinity. Hence, we shall find joy in Jesus while we live here on earth, because in Him we find the Trinity. And since Jesus acts on our souls through the Sacraments, and we enter into His great action on Calvary through Holy Mass, the Sacraments and Holy Mass are intimately connected with our joy. We must therefore, habituate ourselves to regarding them as contacts with Jesus and through Him with the Blessed Trinity, in Whom is our beatitude.

More than that, in the present order of things we may and must give Our Lady a place in our joy analogous to, though completely dependent on, that which belongs to Jesus. Jesus Himself, executing the eternal plan of the Blessed Trinity, gave her to us as our mother. Her mothering is not simply a matter of providing encouragement, or support, or spiritual delicacies. It has to do with our birth to grace and our growth in grace and our eventual union with the Eternal Father in the great family of the elect. Hence, in Mary also we find the Blessed Trinity. And if we joy in her we joy in Them. In the litany of Loreto we address her as "Cause of our Joy". That she is through having given us Jesus and, through Him, the Blessed Trinity. That she is also as Mediatrix of all graces. That she is, finally, in her own person. For just as in the natural order we find joy in many friendships and not only in the unique friendship of our father and mother, so also, in the supernatural order, God wishes us to find joy not in Himself only, and not in Jesus only, but also in all those whose eminent and triumphant grace makes contact with them a glorious and vitalizing experience. These are the saints, among whom Mary, Queen of the Saints and our Mother, occupies a unique place.

It is unfortunate that this elementary fact is at times obscured by narrow and formalistic views. The unique position of the Blessed Trinity in the christian life is in no way endangered by devotion to Our Lady and the saints. Catholic doctrine as crystallized at the time of the so-called Reformation makes that clear even to those who may be unaware of its acceptance in the Church from the earliest times. True, one may err by excess in devotion to saints. But it is possible to err by defect also. And between the two extremes there is room for a wide diversity of practice which every Catholic must recognize as the right of his fellow-catholic, whether at home or in other lands.

* * * *

Coming now to infused joy, obviously there is only a very limited and improper sense in which one can speak of a technique of growth in it. As found in the normal christian life, infused joy is but the accompaniment of a life lived under the influence of grace. God may, for His inscrutable reasons, allow it to find greater or less expression. It is in a somewhat similar way that He allows some virtues to manifest themselves more or less than others in a particular saint, even though the substance of all the virtues is given him with grace. The virtue of magnificence—that virtue which enables a man to undertake schemes involving vast material resources in a worthy manner—cannot be detected in action in the life of our Blessed Lord. But it was in His soul, and could have sprung to action had circumstances so demanded. The case of joy in the average soul is similar—though not of course identical. The grace we all receive from God includes the mechanism of joy. But its operation depends on Him, moving it by actual grace. Hence though we all have the substance of joy within us, we may experience more or less of it. What depends on us is, first of all, to remove those obstacles to joy and growth in grace which we have considered already and then, in the second place, through the spiritual quality of our lives and the outlook which we foster, to facilitate growth in grace and to develop a manner of thinking and willing and doing which God normally blesses with joy. A third and most important aid to growth in infused joy is humble and patient prayer. Joy is a grace, that is to say a favour which can come from God's hand and from no other source. Graces are won by prayer: they are often withheld till they have been prayed for. Joy is of the greatest importance. It is well worth praying for.

It cannot be overstressed however that infused joy, in the sense of joy which proceeds more from what God does in us than from what we do with and under God, is a normal part of a normal christian life. We must all be deeply convinced that there are well-springs of joy within us and that granted the necessary conditions they will inundate our souls. Praying for joy is not praying for something new and additional: it is praying for the release of something given to us already but held in check within us. I have mentioned that the infused element in joy helps to give meaning to what could else be "acting-as-if", as when, in spite of lack of devotion, we elicit acts of joy in God or thank Him for His great glory. In the same way we provide it with an opportunity of welling up in our souls when we turn in prayer to the Blessed Trinity, or think of Jesus' love for us, of His triumphant Resurrection and Ascension, of Mary's immaculate and loving heart, of her queenly dignity and power. In all such prayer joy results not only from our conscious effort, aided by grace, to establish contact with the great supernatural causes of our joy, but also from the action of the Holy Ghost within us: "But the fruit of the Spirit is. . . . . joy, peace. . . ." [5] His action, within the normal framework of the christian life, is conditioned by the orientation we give our souls. If we turn towards the Causes of our joy, He will give joy from within. If we neglect to do so, He is grieved and His action is fettered.[6]

The part which we can play in preparing for growth in infused joy is illustrated by our Blessed Lord in the words "And no man putteth new wine into old bottles . . . . . but new wine must be put into new bottles".[7] He had been questioned about the disconcerting neglect by His desciples of the practice of fasting. His answer was two-fold. Taking up the point raised and treating it first in its own narrow context, He explained that whereas the disciples did not fast while the joy of His presence dominated their lives, a time for fasting would come when He would be taken from them. That done, He proceeded to show the deeper implications of the problem. The new wine of discipleship simply could not, in any case, be preserved in the old bottles of Pharisaical observances, nor even in those of the Baptist's teaching. What the Pharisees did or what John the Baptist did was irrelevant to the way of life He taught. He taught something new, gave a new spirit,

---

[5]Gal. 5, 2.
[6]I have discussed this in more detail in THY KINGDOM COME, in the chapter, The Peace of the Kingdom.
[7]Mk. 2, 22.

7

and that spirit could be received only through a rebirth: the old man must be reshaped before the new spirit could find expression.

Therein is our part made clear. We must provide the new bottles which will contain the joy and peace of the Holy Ghost. His joy and peace cannot pervade a life lived according to the spirit of fallen man. Only in a restricted measure can they pervade a life which christianity rules merely to the extent of inspiring a certain respect for duty.[8] Joy and peace of the Holy Ghost will be ours to the extent to which we put on the new man of a total change of mind in Christ. They are normally denied us to the extent to which we cling to the old man of fallen nature.

Earlier in this chapter we spoke of the work to be done in freeing ourselves from the attachments that hamper this life of grace in the soul. This work opens the soul to infused joy for it is, in effect, part of our effort to co-operate with God in the formation of the new man within us. The same is true of all that has been said, and will yet be said, about growth in the christian outlook and in the christian virtues. For our present purpose it will therefore be sufficient to refer briefly to some practices which aid the process of change into the mind of Christ, making of us new bottles in which the new wine of christian joy and peace may be held.[9]

In the first place we may seek entry into the mind of Christ through contact with Him in the liturgical year. The liturgical year presents Jesus to us in His essential features, and, linked as it is with the Blessed Eucharist, it has a

---

[8]There is no implication here that a sense of duty is an unimportant thing. Keeping the commandments is the surest sign of the love of God. But an adequate sense of our duty to God means more than to believe that if we keep certain commandments, the rest of our lives belongs to ourselves. For the new man in Christ, duty is fused with love rather than love narrowed down to the sphere of strict duty.

[9]The three practices selected for mention here are in no sense exhaustive. Their special importance lies in their sacramental or quasi-sacramental efficacy.

special power to reproduce within us what it represents. Briefly, it shows us God-made-man, come on earth for us men and for the Father's glory, suffering and dying in the performance of His work, but triumphing over death and sin and now throned glorious and triumphant. From Heaven He sends the Holy Ghost to enlighten and guide the Church and to dwell in the hearts of His members. The ultimate goal of our incorporation in His Mystical Body and our inhabitation by the Holy Ghost is recalled in the great feast of the Blessed Trinity. Coming to Jesus year by year within this cycle we learn to know Him as the Lamb who is King of Kings and Lord of Lords,[10] in Whom we have access in One Spirit to the Father,[11] in Whom all things are made new.[12] This is a heart-warming and inspiring knowledge of Jesus that reveals the total meaning of life and reduces its problems to their due proportions.

In the second place we may seek entry to His mind through Holy Mass, guided by the Church's liturgical text. And here the most significant point is the Church's insistence on thanksgiving, following St. Mark's ". . . and having taken the chalice, giving thanks He gave it to them".[13] Thanksgiving was an immensely important part in Jesus' adoration of His Father. He knew the Father as the fount of all good—good given and good to come. He approached the Father His heart full of gratitude and laid down His life in gratitude. We put on the mind of Christ when to Holy Mass we bring the recollection of all that God has done for us, most of all what He has done for us in His Divine Son—mindful, in the words of the Canon of the Mass, of the Passion, Resurrection and Glorious Ascension of Christ. Those who are drawn to God by a gratitude which is a sharing in Jesus' gratitude will offer themselves to Him

---

[10]Apoc. 19, 16.
[11]Eph. 2, 18.
[12]Apoc. 21, 5.
[13]Mk. 14, 23.

gladly as victims. Their daily lives will be lightened by the conviction that God has been unspeakably good to them and to all souls. God did not make service a condition of His loving ". . . not as though we had loved God, but because He hath first loved us".[14] He wishes our homage to spring from knowledge of the debt of love we bear Him.

In the last place we may seek entry to the mind of Christ in Holy Communion. Holy Communion is the transforming sacrament, the one in which Jesus works to change us into Himself. From it ultimately we hope for growth in likeness to Him and in union with Him. Made like Him in Holy Communion, His Spirit will find freedom to dwell in us in something of the fulness in which He dwelt in Jesus. The Holy Ghost dwelt in Jesus as the Spirit of joy.[15] To Jesus, received in Holy Communion, we turn that through the gift of His Spirit we may share in His joy.

God is love: God is beatitude. He gives Himself to us as He is in Himself. Hence, there is always joy in His gifts, even when they are crosses.

---

[14]I Jo. 4, 10.
[15]cf. Luke 10, 21.

7

JOY IN SUFFERING

MADE for happiness, and yearning with our whole hearts for it, we cannot achieve it fully during our time of spiritual growth on earth. In the very nature of things happiness on earth cannot but be imperfect. Final happiness is in the vision of God, which is attained through the doorway of death. And right up to the moment of death, the soul is susceptible of spiritual development, each new stage being more perfect than the relatively imperfect one which preceded it, and all being immeasurably less perfect than the final stage of glory.

The imperfection of human spiritual happiness is not, therefore, in its every aspect, a consequence of the Fall. Even had Adam never sinned perfect happiness would be ours only in heaven. But the Fall has contributed in many ways to making the happiness which we are likely to attain to on earth much less full than it would have been. Sickness and pain have entered life. The harmony of man's faculties has been disturbed. Man suffers both from his fellow man and from unsympathetic forces of nature. And underlying all these different sources of suffering, there is suffering in the very manner of his spiritual growth. The cross does not remain wholly outside him. His way of carrying it is hesitant, and a source of self-reproach. There is darkness and doubt in his understanding of spiritual things. Only with difficulty can he throw the full energy of his will into life. His sensibility is subject to fear and depression. These are the commonplaces cf any explanation of the effects of Original Sin. Taken all together they mount up to a significant total of inescapable pain. More than that, they show the range of the limitations of our happiness, limitations which follow not only from the imperfect nature of the happiness itself, but also from its co-existence within one soul with so much pain.

Jesus' beatific joy was not susceptible of diminution during His earthly life. Hence, there is no exact parallel between the problem of joy in suffering in His life and in ours. On the other hand, He did truly suffer, and suffered most acutely: His soul was capable of sorrow even unto death. From that point of view there is a parallel, and for us a most consoling one, between His way and ours of tasting sorrow with joy. Joy could not be driven out of His life. But pain could be introduced into it. And to that He agreed, willing in all things to be like us, sin only excepted. Any treatment of the problem of joy and suffering must, therefore begin with gratitude to Jesus Who, in love for us and in His desire to be near us, gave pain an entry to His life which it need not have had. More than that, He gave us a joy which though less perfect than His, shares in a real, even if partial manner, in the power of His joy to withstand the onslaught of pain. With His help, our joy can have the firmness of charity, from which ultimately it springs: "Many waters cannot quench charity, neither can the floods drown it."[1] He became like to us in the pain He suffered, and has willed that we be like Him in the relatively indestructible quality He gives our joy. Even now, on the threshold of the problem, our debt of gratitude weighs heavy on us.

*   *   *   *

We see therefore in Jesus that the presence of pain in life is not an unmixed evil: there is room for gratitude in our acceptance of it. And this idea leads at once to a point which is fundamental to the very possibility of growth in spiritual joy: the acceptance of pain as a fact, and as a fact of spiritual significance. There can be no question of joy in suffering if

[1]Cant. 8, 7.

suffering is not reckoned and admitted among the factors that make up life and contribute to its fulness.

In the first place, to accept pain as a fact. On paper pain may appear an obvious fact of life. In actual living one may regard it at every encounter as something that ought not to have been at all. There is all that difference between theory and practice in even the same man. In some unconscious way we have what may be described as a racial memory and hankering after the conditions of life in Eden, we are drawn to happiness and want it now. We recoil instinctively from pain and want nothing of it. And so we tend, without perhaps being aware of what we are doing, to draw up a practical philosophy of life with pain left out. Not that our philosophy is deliberately unchristian: on the contrary many a truly christian principle goes to its formulation. But it is always defective, always being reworded in the light of experience. And one of its common defects is that pain does not figure at all in it, or is given only a grudged place. Such an attitude to pain obviously rules out spiritual joy to a greater or less degree from our moments of suffering. And since the spiritual life is all of one piece, it will be an obstacle to joy even outside them. We cannot deliberately shirk any of life's issues hoping to deal with the rest entirely on their own merits.

In the second place, we must accept pain as a fact of spiritual significance, that is to say, as a factor which contributes directly or indirectly to spiritual growth. This is more than accepting pain as a fact. It means welcoming pain. And yet it is more akin to accepting pain as fact than might at first appear. For when we examine the problem of pain, the ultimate difficulty in it is this: that God freely allowed pain into the world whereas He might have excluded it. True, we can see reasons why pain was allowed. But we also see that it could have been dispensed with. We admit that God in His Wisdom sees a picture of pain's fruitfulness which fully justifies it. But we see that picture only imperfectly, and in the same imperfect way see possibilities of a painless world. In the last resort, then, to accept pain as spiritually significant reduces itself to an act of faith: I believe in the value of pain in this present world because a wise and loving God allows it to be. Pain is a spiritually significant fact which need not have been a fact at all. Our deepest recognition of its value is to accept it in faith from God's hands.

This is not of course to say that theology can make no useful contribution to a discussion of the problem of pain. Theology can intervene most effectively at two points. The first is during the consideration of pain in itself and antecedently to its permission by God. At this point theology can show that there is nothing intrinsically incongruous in allowing pain to be. The second point is while examining the advantages and disadvantages of the pain that has been allowed into this present world. Here theology helps us by showing the various ways in which pain, the evil, is channelled into good. But it will be noted that in between these two points lies the crucial one: the point at which we consider that God freely selected a world with pain rather than a painless one. There we are up against the mystery of God's freedom, and theology can do no more than to say that God's freedom is ordered by His Wisdom. God has allowed pain to be a fact. In doing so He was Wise and Good and Merciful. We cannot see how His Wisdom and Goodness and Mercy found it more appropriate to manifest Themselves in the permission of pain rather than in its exclusion. We have only faith to lead us to accept-ance. Each time we experience it pain comes to us as a fact that might never have been, and we are called to accept it in faith, and through faith in trust and love and joyous assent.

*   *   *   *

Thus, underlying our acceptance of pain there must be an attitude of unquestioning submission to the reality of

God's love for us and the deep wisdom of the choice He made of the way by which we must draw near to Him. On that attitude as foundation we can begin to build up joy. While pain is questioned, joy is impossible or at best fragmentary.

Joy does not, of course, spring from the experience of pain itself. Only a perverted sensibility finds pain a pleasure-yielding experience and one to be sought or induced for its own sake. What joy there is in our experience of pain springs always from the fact that certain virtues are called into play by it. The exercise of these virtues is accompanied by joy: the pain remains pain. One of the virtues so called into play is faith. For pain invites us to turn our minds in faith to God's Wisdom and Mercy, to the love Jesus bears us, to the motherly way in which Mary intervenes that we be not tried beyond our limited powers of endurance. Such contact with God, with Jesus and with Mary in faith is productive of spiritual joy and this joy blunts the sharp edge of pain. Hope is called into play also: we endure pain relying on grace and looking forward to an eternal reward. Charity is there too: we accept pain in love as something coming, however mysteriously, from the hand of our Father in Heaven. Together with these theological virtues, certain moral virtues may be exercised, such as patience which helps us to bear courageously the sorrow which pain causes and perseverance which strengthens the soul to endure difficulties that persist over a long time, and other similar virtues belonging to the general category of fortitude. All these virtues, like the theological ones, have joy attached to their exercise and so contribute to strengthening the soul to bear the pain incidental to the christian life.

St. Thomas, with his customary thoroughness and clarity, treats of the question of the joy experienced in the exercise of the virtue of fortitude.[2] What he says throws an invaluable

---

[2] IIa IIae, Q 123, a 8.

light on the problem, and it is well worth while to consider it here.

He points out that fortitude, as does every virtue, yields joy in its exercise. But it does so in circumstances peculiar to itself. For its exercise may be occasioned by bodily pain, or by spiritual pain, or by both together.

This does not obtain with the other virtues, which may be exercised in circumstances involving no special difficulty, as for example, when a person is drawn to love of God or his neighbour without experiencing at that particular moment the need to manifest it by some painful sacrifice. Hence, the joy of fortitude always finds itself offset by pain, and the pain is capable of dulling the perception of joy. Normally, he tells us, and unless God intervenes by a special grace, the brave christian does not find joy outweighing pain. The virtue of fortitude can normally achieve no more than to save the soul from being oppressed and borne down by pain. He quotes with approval the dictum of Aristotle that it is sufficient if the brave man does not give way to sorrow, even if he cannot find it within himself to experience interior joy.

In the course of his discussion St. Thomas stresses the point that acts of virtue yield joy especially through the motive for which they are performed. It is therefore consistent with his teaching to hold that when pain is endured for motives of faith, hope and charity, the joy which springs from the acts of these virtues is something over and above the joy which springs from the mere act of fortitude considered in itself. Hence it may well happen that in bearing sufferings of a moderate kind a christian will find that his joy dominates his pain when his faith, hope and charity are intense, and this without any special grace being given him. But where suffering is intense his experience of joy may be blotted out. This does not, however, mean to say that pain will rule his soul; rather, that joy is consumed in making pain bearable. If the terminology be permitted, we may say that in such circumstances joy is transformed into peace, and pain is borne in peace. His joy, even though he is not conscious of it, works secretly in his soul and strengthens him to bear his pain in a tranquil and ordered way. It safeguards him against futile rebelling, impatience and loss of spiritual poise. He suffers, but without wavering in his attitude to life. He is on the cross, but as one who by God's grace can reign there, and not as a frustrated and tortured victim.

"When a strong man armed keepeth his court, those things are in peace which he possesseth".[3] The christian's great personal possession is a soul united in love with God. To keep that possession intact he needs strength. Not a strength that is never tested, but a strength that can win through in the time of testing. Part of his strength is joy. During his mortal life joy is not given him by God only that he may taste its sweetness, but also that it may help him to endure the bitterness of pain in peace, a peace which no pain can take away.

*   *   *   *

In the text of St. Thomas to which reference has been made above, we are reminded of the importance of the motive in determining the joy which accompanies an act of virtue. Truthfulness, for example, yields its own proper joy. But still more is joy found in telling truth for the love of God. For the reasons already given, the role of the motive is of special importance in bearing pain with christian courage (or fortitude). Hence it will be profitable to consider some of the motives for courageous action which a christian may invoke in the time of trial.

The first is St. Paul's "For I reckon that the sufferings of this time are not worthy to be compared with the glory to come that shall be revealed in us"[4] Suffering is to be borne in hope. We look forward with serene confidence to eternal glory. Nothing that happens to us in life is, of itself, capable

---

[3]Lk. 11, 21.
[4]Rom. 8, 18.

of disturbing our movement towards that goal. Suffering even contributes to it, if borne in love of God. With beatitude clear, inviting and attainable on our horizons, the momentary trials of any particular stage in our journey seem of little account.

It is not foreign to the spirit of St. Paul's words to remind ourselves that many of the sufferings which we consider hard to bear, are, by any reckoning—and not only in comparison with the glory to come—of little account. Any indulgence in self-pity destroys our sense of proportion in regard to pain. Viewed exclusively in relation to ourselves any trial at all is intolerable—at least in the sense of being completely unwelcome. In itself it may be but a trifle and less still if compared with what others endure without complaint. It is nothing at all when weighed against the eternal reward. And yet we can magnify it into a heavy burden by considering it exclusively in its effects on self, reacting to it almost as if pain had never been experienced by any human being till we appeared on the scene. We need a sense of proportion in judging the true dimensions of our trials. We need also a keen sense of the proportion any particular trial bears to the joy of eternal life. Often enough before considering any of the motives for bearing a trial, we ought first to ask ourselves the question: is the trial big enough to justify our training a battery of heavy motives on it, or is the better thing to make a simple and loving act of acceptance and then try to dismiss it from our minds?

Love of God is another powerful motive for enduring suffering. There may, however, be some practical difficulty about seeing how exactly to integrate love into our endurance. To take a simple example: how does one bear a headache for love of God?

One thinks easily enough of negative ways of doing so. We may show our love of God by not murmuring against Him, by not complaining, by not giving way to irritation and impatience. But all these are forms of not acting rather than forms of acting, and hence there is nothing in them from which joy may follow. On the other hand, a positive act of acceptance of the headache as something allowed by God for wise and merciful reasons followed up by offering it to Him in union with the great sufferings of Our Blessed Lord, would be an exercise of virtue—of many virtues in fact—and could therefore be joyous. But it could hardly be sustained. It is rather something to be done and then committed, as it were to God's memory. The truth is that bearing a headache in love is a much more simple thing than that and can be kept up while the headache lasts. It is to keep on loving Him even though one has a headache: that is to say, to keep on doing what is His holy will at the moment, in spite of the temptation to abandon all effort and sink into self-pity. Thus, a person suffering from a headache bears it in love if he continues to do his work, if he keeps at his prayers, if he deals charitably with his neighbour, and so on. The joy of all those acts of love make the headache at least more bearable, and offering it to God in love amounts to something no more difficult than not to allow it to divert us from His love. This example over-simplifies the problem of suffering to some extent, but at least it indicates quite clearly the direction in which to look for an explanation of how love accepts and eases pain. No less clearly it shows that pain is not "offered up" to God precisely by concentrating on it and holding ourselves in a sustained attitude of patient acceptance.

*   *   *   *

Those who suffer are aided to bear their suffering by the possibility it opens to them of sharing in a special way in Jesus' redemptive work. Here they find another motive which, accepted in faith and love, becomes a source of joy and peace.

Redemption is complete in Jesus. In Him are saved all who will be saved: in Him they have triumphed over sin and death. But the completeness of the Redemption Jesus wrought does not exclude us men from contributing in some way to the redemption of our fellow-men. Jesus is willing to grant us a real title to a share in the saving efficacy of His sacred Passion and Death. He is willing that the saving grace which flows from Him to souls may reach them as in some way ours also if we have entered into union with Him in His saving action. This we can do by any meritorious act which we offer for souls through Him. But most particularly we can do so when what we offer is suffering borne in union with Him suffering. Our sufferings do not add to the efficacy of His. What they do is to entitle us to claim as ours some of the fruits of His sufferings, not by a merely empty claim, but by one grounded in our real union with Him and His desire to admit those so united with Him deep into the riches of His glorifying love of the Father and His saving love of men.

Viewed in this light, suffering is more than a personal experience, even though a valuable and purifying one. It is something done to change the course of the world of souls, something done to save men and thereby give glory to God. One of the great temptations that assail us in the time of suffering is to regard it as an interruption of worth-while activity. A missionary is forced home by ill-health, a lay apostle finds himself misunderstood and opposed, a young mother finds herself left the sole support of an infant child— they all feel that the life they were living for God and the things they were doing for Him have come to an end, and that only when the trial will have passed or a solution to it found will it be possible once more to make a positive contribution to God's glory and the good of souls. They tend to forget that the whole of the possible positive contribution has been made already by Jesus. All we can do, whether in joy or in suffering, is to enter into His labours. The missionary in his work, the lay-apostle in his courageous initiative, the mother in training her child, are all drawing on Jesus' merits and saving power: the good they do is done by Him through them. He can continue to do that same good through them if their contribution is changed into suffering. Only the visible framework of the cause and effect relationship will be different. They will be as truly forces for good in the one case as in the other. Suffering does not interrupt our spiritual fruitfulness: all it does is to change its form or its way of working.

Those who suffer will find a special joy in offering up their sufferings for the success of the active labours of others who toil in fields from which they are themselves debarred. Thus, a missionary forced home by ill-health may offer that trial to God as a sacrifice to win grace for active missionaries throughout the world and for the souls they evangelize. Doing so helps him to feel that his apostolate has not come to an end. It is now more spiritual, more selfless, no less real—perhaps more real. A person harassed by temptation can ask God to accept his anguish as the price of the salvation of sinners trembling on the brink of despair. A bereaved wife can implore God to console the lonely and abandoned as she would wish to be consoled. This is to imitate Jesus Who saved us by His pain: to imitate Our Father in heaven Who accepted the death of His Divine Son as the redeeming price of souls. The more we ponder on it the more evident it becomes that in all fittingness there can be no redemption without the shedding of blood. A redeemer must be one in all things like to those he would save. No one can save the wavering, the over-burdened, the suffering, more appropriately than those who freely accept to be placed by God in similar trials and freely offer them to Him as a saving sacrifice through Jesus. "For we have not a high priest who can have compassion on our infirmities; but one tempted in all things like as we are, without sin".[5]

The motive of reparation also comes to mind at this point. One aspect of it is particularly relevant. Much of the sin in the world is due to a refusal to accept the cross. Despair, drunkenness, sexual vice, blasphemy—these are but a few of the sins in which men seek vain relief from pain. It is fitting that for pain rejected reparation be made by pain accepted. The fittingness is not of the mathematical kind, as if a certain amount of sin must be balanced by an equal amount of the opposed virtue. It lies rather in

---

[5]Hebr. 4, 15.

the fact that glory is due to God, and love and reverence urge us to give Him all of it that is His due. Every refusal to accept pain is so much glory denied Him. If we love Him we shall try to welcome the pain which comes our way so that the total of the world's hymn of glory to Him be filled up. In thus making reparation we think not so much of the sinner who has offended God, as of God Who has been offended. Perhaps there may be some slight danger of self-complacency in harbouring the idea of making good the defects of others. There is none in trying to love God with one's whole heart and soul and giving Him the glory of which He has been deprived. And what a cheering thing it is to feel one is doing something so pleasing to God and so fully expressive of a love sensitive to His interests.

* * * *

A great part of the secret of finding joy in pain is to turn away from oneself to God and to others. Some of the ways in which this may be done by our interior attitude have been considered. There remains the question of giving this attitude external expression. It is an important one. For an attitude, unless it is given external expression, is likely to hover between willing and mere wishing, and is likely enough to cease after a time to have any real value.

The eighth Station of the Cross, which is based on a text of St. Luke[6] presents us with a wonderful example of self-forgetful suffering. Jesus is bearing His Cross. He is weak as a result of the barbarous treatment of the previous hours and already so near to death as to have caused His executioners anxiety lest He might die before reaching Calvary. He meets a group of people, among whom were many women, who were touched with pity at His plight. He spoke to them. But never a word of His sufferings, never a suspicion that He seized on their sympathy as an excuse to win still more from them. His mind is filled

---

[6]Lk. 23, 27-31.

rather with the thought of what they will have to suffer: ". . . weep not over me; but weep for yourselves and for your children". Borne down by the Cross, His heart bleeds for them—they who were sinners and the cause of His death.

Unless we make a conscious effort to keep the needs of others uppermost in our minds there is a very real danger that suffering will embitter us. Suffering tends to bring the self into clamorous prominence, and once the mind turns to self it risks losing interest in anything outside self: once it lingers on the wrongs endured by self it is on the way to hostile indifference to the rights and feelings of others. Suffering is not a sacrament. It does not work *ex opere operato*. It is an opportunity, and a most valuable one, of becoming Christlike. Alone, however, and without our contribution it does not change us for the better: rather does it, by its very nature, tend to change us for the worse.

Hence those who suffer should feel themselves invited by grace to charity and sympathy towards their neighbour. St. Paul says of every high priest that he must be one who can have compassion on them that are ignorant and that err, because he himself also is encompassed with infirmity. Suffering is intended to open the heart to compassion and sympathy. One who suffers ought to appreciate better than anyone else the need of the human heart for help and encouragement. Suffering is, therefore, an experience which, with the help of God's grace, is calculated to enlarge the heart, to open it to men and to schemes for the good and the salvation of men. One who has never suffered may perhaps never learn just how much a man needs help. His horizons remain narrow: he sees but a part of what can be done in a lifetime. Never having laboured in pain he remains undeveloped in his experience of the joy that is found in serving and saving others.

It is therefore a matter of great practical importance that

---

[7] Hebr. 5, 2.

8

during a time of suffering a christian pay more than usual heed to the claims which others have on his service and sympathy and charity. To do this will help him by taking his mind to some extent off himself. It will help him by the joy in which he will find in his charity. It will help him also by the way in which his sympathy will lead others to confide in him and give him a glimpse of sufferings far greater, perhaps, than his own which they bear in secret. It will help him finally by deepening his spiritual life and so increasing his capacity for joy: for a life which is devoted in spite of personal pain to the good of God's children is a deeply spiritual one, in which is established a true hierarchy of values and effort is directed into truly profitable channels. Saints on their death-beds have been more concerned about the loss of sleep and other cares they caused their nurses than about themselves. For them suffering was hardly suffering. At least it was not a thing to be distressed about. If we can, let us look on our cross more as a means of saving others and an invitation to save them than as a thing to be fitted into the pattern of our own salvation. By losing our life for others we save it: by putting ourselves in the first place we lose much and risk losing all.

* * * *

Joy in suffering is a possibility. It becomes all the more possible the less we allow suffering to make us preoccupied with self. Peace in suffering is the normal thing for one who is leading a good christian life: there is no reason to fear that any suffering allowed by God will take away our peace of soul. Let us, however, understand quite clearly what this peace is: not something which makes us insensible to suffering or takes away its power to pain us, but that condition of soul which results from acceptance of God's holy will, no matter how difficult acceptance may be. Where there is acceptance there is peace. Where there is peace there may yet, by God's mercy, be joy.

8

PROVIDENCE AND JOY

A FREQUENT cause of anxiety in life is the feeling that things are not happening according to any rational plan. Our Blessed Lord noted this as one of the trials men will endure at the end of the world: " . . . men withering away for fear and expectation of what shall come upon the whole world".[1] Not only fear of what has happened and of what is happening, but fear of what may happen will cause men to wither. Though this fear will in a special way mark the last stretches of time, it is not confined to them. Men always tend to fear what may happen, even more than what is happening. Into the disasters of today they read the still greater disasters of the morrow. And whereas they find within them the courage to face the dangers they can see, the unnamed dangers of the future fill them with blank dread.

To counteract this fear as well as to give us reason for joy God has revealed to us the fact of Divine Providence. God who drew all things from nothingness by an act of His Will, and without Whom nothing can be or pass from one stage of existence or activity to another, fashioned this universe according to a plan. He did not work experimentally, making things to be and then seeing how they would shape. It would be metaphysically impossible for Him to do so. Not even in the slightest detail of its structure or workings could the universe be independent of Him, for He is the unique ultimate source of all being and all activity and without Him can be

---

[1] Lk. 21, 26.

nothing that is or that acts. Nor in any case could He, Who is Wisdom, have created a universe without a purpose. God could not be God and at the same time act aimlessly. All that He made, all that in His making He allowed to be, could not but be part of a Divine plan, made to be or allowed to be in view of the plan's realization.

St. Paul tells us what was God's final purpose in making the world as we now know it. It was ". . . in the fulness of times, to re-establish all things in Christ, that are in Heaven and earth . . .".[2] St. Paul's thought does not stop at the Redemption, which was a true re-establishment of all things in Christ, even though made effective only in the course of time. Had his thought stopped there we might fear—however unreasonably—that with Jesus' Ascension into Heaven and the sending of the Holy Ghost God's purpose had been attained and the course of events thereafter would, in some sense, be a matter of indifference. God's purpose looked forward to the final re-establishment of all things in Christ in eternity and therefore embraced every event preceding it. That St. Paul had eternity in mind is clear from that other striking text, "And when all things shall be subdued unto Him (that is, to Jesus), then the Son also Himself shall be subject unto him that put all things under him, that God may be all in all".[3] The final term of God's providential action is all things re-established in Christ, and through Him brought back to the Trinity. From God we came. For God we are destined. The end of this world is the elect gathered up in Christ and introduced through Him into the bosom of the Trinity.

It would lead us too far afield to consider how in St. Paul's thought even the brute, vegetable and inanimate creation are included among the "all things" that are to be subdued to Jesus. It is sufficient to note that he has man most particularly in mind. But because man, and each individual man, is influenced in his return to God in Christ by the impact of his material milieu, this also is included—at least obliquely—in

---

[2]Eph. 1, 10.
[3]I Cor. 15, 28.

God's providential ordering of the world. Thus each one of us can say that the whole world, the whole universe, in which he finds himself, is a planned and plan-regulated unit. We know by faith the final stage of the plan. Its path of realization has not been revealed to us. But we have no doubt of its sureness. Left in darkness about the way God has chosen, we see in the certain light of faith that some sure way has been chosen by Him and that it leads most certainly to the goal of His choice.

God's Providence extends to each individual soul as well as to the world of souls. Just as each individual soul is brought into being by a special divine action, and each individual soul is sanctified by a special divine action, so also each individual soul has its own place determined for it from all eternity within the bosom of the Godhead. In Christ we are predestined for the Beatific Vision, each one of us as well as all of us. The little world of each one of us is ordered to an end—the eternal good of our soul—no less than the whole universe. There is no more chaos in the world of any soul than in the totality of God's creation. For God's Wisdom is infinite and reaches to the details of the life of the individual no less than to the details of the organization of all things in Christ. But while it is always necessary to insist on the fact that a particular providence rules the lives of each of the elect, it is perhaps more necessary today to stress the general Providence which rules the building up of the Body of Christ unto the perfection of eternity. For chaos reigns or threatens to reign in the world. And the individual feels himself threatened not so much by his own setting as by the wider setting by which all men's lives are bounded. Nor is this the only reason for turning to Providence's wider horizons. It is heartening to realize that God has a plan in Christ which is of world-wide dimensions and which cannot fail in its execution. Admittedly it is a wonderful thing to know that God has provided for my future. But is it not more wonderful still to know that He has provided for the future of the whole world? Does not what He is prepared to do for me seem more by the simple fact that it is being done by One Who can and will provide for the countless host of the elect? God deals with His creation in a manner worthy of Himself. He cares for souls more as befits Him than as they deserve. Keeping that idea before our minds, trust and joy in Providence become almost natural to us.

*   *   *   *

Strictly speaking Providence is on the intellectual level: it is God's intellectual grasp of the end for which He made things and of their ordered progress towards it. Corresponding to Providence there is, on the level of will, what we may term the Divine government of the world. God did not rest with having a plan, He put it into execution. God's government of the world is His execution of the plan conceived by His Providence. Speaking above of Providence we have of necessity touched on government also. Though quite distinct as ideas, in treatment they tend to shade over one into the other.

In regard to the Divine government of souls the point I should like most particularly to make—and it will be seen to be valid for providence also—is that God guides souls as their Father. God sees us, sees the world of souls, in Jesus, His Divine Son. Souls share by grace in Jesus' Sonship. God's care of us is fatherly. And, as Tertullian so beautifully put it, who is so much a father as God is? When St. John tells us that God is love, his words have a very particular application here. God deals with us in a loving way. What He sends comes from a Father's hand. What He allows is allowed by a Father. All, both what is sent and what is allowed, comes as part of the process leading up to the attainment of the end God has proposed for us. God, we may say, is an ambitious father in what concerns us His children. He has destined us for something incredibly big and never ceases to guide us towards it. We, for our part, place all our confidence in His guidance.

From the fact that God governs the world in the interests of souls it does not, of course, follow that He will never allow us to experience a spiritual set-back. God's eye is on the final goal. Ours is mostly on the intermediate stages. That is why we so often find God's leading hard to understand and accept. We think out, as we must, what to do and what to undertake in His service, and to our disappointment—if not to our disillusionment—find that we fail. We feel that we have failed in more than the thing attempted: we feel that it was a failure in life, a failure that will hold us up short of the goal we could have achieved had we succeeded in it. And in this we are most likely wrong: wrong, whether our failure was due to ourselves or to circumstances outside us. For we simply cannot know the detailed stages by which we are to find our way to union with the Trinity in Christ. It may be that our culpable failures have been permitted by God as a stage in our way to Him, for He is so good and so powerful that out of evil He can win good. Admittedly, we were not moving towards Him at the very moment when we failed Him. But that failure, and the many failures to follow, may yet one day by His grace, contribute to work in us a miracle of true conversion like that which transformed St. Augustine's soul. The world, too, may at times veer right or left of the way that leads to its ultimate purpose. But it has not, for all that, escaped the Father's merciful control. He Who sees all time in a single glance allows it to deviate only as much as He has foreseen. And that deviation He will provide for at some future moment which is His secret. Hence, failures, both real and apparent, in the life of the individual and in the winning of the world for God, are not a reason for losing peace of soul. Even if real, a failure may be God's way of marking a stage in ultimate success. As for apparent failures, how many of what pass for failures are such only on the surface and provide no grounds whatever for sadness or despair. If only we could form the habit of seeing life whole, or rather, of seeing that life is a whole of which only a minute part is at any moment being lived by us, our passing triumphs and failures would be valued at their true significance. There would be less empty glorying and less vain regrets. God sees life whole. We may share in His joy by seeing life in His vision.

*   *   *   *

Do we appreciate sufficiently the idea that life is a whole and must be judged as such? It has been one of the secondary themes of this book that life in time and in eternity forms an organic unity. We cannot judge truly the weight to attach to any occurrence in our life in time if we do not make allowance for the eternity that is to follow. We are familiar with the idea that we have not here a lasting city, but look towards one that is to come: that we are on a journey while in this world. But nonetheless we insist on judging every rise or fall in our condition in time as if it were to endure for ever. A man on a journey does not attach the same importance to bad food and lodgings as he would to the same food and accommodation if they were offered him at home. He knows the journey will come to an end. Home he looks on as going to stay. And that simple difference of transiency and permanence can make the same trial bearable in one case and insupportable in the other. All our trials in this world are stamped with transiency. The really significant thing in life is not what is happening now but the direction God gives it by grace. And that direction is not always evident, does not always appear straight. God Who loves us asks that our dealings with Him in time be in faith. And that too is but a passing phase, for, seen whole, our contacts with Him are preponderantly in vision, since such are the contacts of eternity.

We may find in the life of Jesus a striking example of the apparently devious way in which God governs the lives of those dear to Him. It has been referred to already in an earlier chapter. Jesus began His work of saving souls by embarking on a life of teaching, supported on the one hand by miracles and on the other by the testimony of the prophets. The beginning of His public life offers the picture of a clearly conceived plan—and one of which the Father approved—put into whole-hearted execution. It met with difficulties. It did not triumph over them. Instead, the difficulties seemed to force a new approach to the problem of man's salvation, and to determine that it would be achieved in a way not included in Jesus' original plan. How like to the occasion when we have to abandon something undertaken for God or for our own spiritual advancement, and are tempted to feel that His government of the world is not, after all, so very effective! Looking back now on Jesus' life in the light of history—a light in which we can see it whole—it is clear to us that the failure of the first approach did not mean failure to reach the goal. God was glorified and men were saved, and that through an initial failure, leading up to what looked like a final failure. As I have said, the truth of the matter is clear to us in history, for history looks back and sees wholes: human agents at the time of acting see only parts. By faith we are given something of history's power to view things in their true perspective: looking, not backward, but forward, we see them as minute parts fitting, we know not how, into a whole which is good as only God can make things good. In a striking passage St. Paul tells us: ". . . let us run by patience to the fight proposed to us; looking on Jesus, the author and finisher of faith, who, having joy set before Him, endured the cross, despising the shame, and now sitteth on the right hand of the throne of God".[4] Jesus saw the cross in the light of eternity. He saw stretching out before Him the unending glory of His triumphant enthronment in heaven. In the same light we must view life. In that light can be seen nothing except what is transformed by eternal joy.

* * * *

Granted then that there is a Divine Providence which covers the universe and each individual soul, and granted also the Divine government of all things and all lives, there arises the practical question: how must I act so as to co-operate with God's guidance of my life? For God's guidance does not force our wills, but we can work more or less in harmony with Him.

The broad lines along which God directs every human life are contained in revelation. In His teaching and in His law-giving God has indicated to every soul the general

---

[4]Hebr. 12, 1-2.

direction He wishes it to give its life, and implicitly He has given it in outline an account of the form His guidance will take. For example, God wishes us to accept the dogmas of the Trinity and the Incarnation and allow them to influence our lives. If we do so, we have the assurance that we are co-operating with Him in tending towards our ultimate goal. Similarly He wishes our lives to be marked by respect for authority, by purity, by a love of justice. Those also are some of the general lines along which He guides us. It is clear, then, that a very great measure of co-operation with Divine Providence is possible for the simplest christian who knows little more than the principal mysteries of religion and the main precepts of the Divine Law. Respecting them in his life he puts himself most effectively under the influence of grace: more effectively, it may be noted, than a much better instructed christian whose obedience to God's commandments falls short of his understanding of advanced theology. The type of christian I have mentioned—and this is true, of course, of any christian who respects God's teaching and His law in daily life—can have the firm conviction that in essentials his life fits into God's providential plan. He is on the sure way that leads to eternal success and even now he can rejoice in the hope of attaining to glory through continued co-operation with God's grace.

God's teaching and God's law are proposed to us for our acceptance by the Church. Hence, we turn to the Church in order to find out what it is fundamentally that God asks of us. But the Church gives us more than the mere essentials of christian living. Guided by the Holy Ghost, she is a living teacher, sensitive to the problems and needs of the age. She does not rest content with offering us her timeless truths and timeless laws in their timeless form. She tells us also what it is that God asks of men here and now. And she does this in varying degrees of authority and persuasiveness by the voice of the Holy Father, by the various Roman Congregations, by the voice of bishops throughout the world. Very frequently these different voices do nothing more than to make explicit what God has already revealed. Such, for example, is the case when a bishop recalls to the minds of his flock the guilt of the sin of injustice or the inspiring dogma of the real presence of Jesus in the Blessed Sacrament, because he sees that these are points which are being forgotten or which may have been questioned. There are times, however, when the Church goes further than that. Guided by the Holy Spirit, though not with that special form of guidance which characterizes her infallible teaching, she elaborates the implications of revelation and, remaining within the spirit of God's teaching, explains to the christian how he may enter into God's designs in his concrete setting of time and place. This she does when, for example, the Holy Father issues an urgent appeal to all to enter more fully into active participation in Catholic action or the missionary movement, pointing out and approving of various practical ways in which this may be done. Clearly there is more in such directives than a mere statement of revelation, or even of what is virtually contained in it. The Holy Father's message is not just the general one that there is a universal call to Catholic action and to missionary activity. He is pin-pointing the call to one of special urgency here and now and indicating ways of answering it. Though not infallible in his reading of the times nor in the concrete methods he judges opportune to suggest, he nevertheless speaks with authority, speaks as the one whom the Holy Spirit has appointed to guide the Church of God. When, therefore, we submit to His guidance, we find ourselves in the current of God's government of the world. And the same is true when we follow the authoritative guidance of our bishop, who holds from God authority to teach and rule within his diocese. It may conceivably happen that the guidance given us does not lead to the results hoped for: one or other of the methods of work proposed may prove inadequate. Whatever of this, most certainly God asks that we respect authority where He has put it. In respecting it we move towards the ultimate goal, even if we fail to reach the intermediate one. But, over and above that, it is important to remember that normally the detailed guidance given by the Church is under every respect right and opportune. When it fails to achieve results, the reason is most likely not that it was defective but that it was insufficiently heeded. To return to the two examples quoted above, how much further would not Catholic Action and missionary activity have advanced throughout the world had the directions of the Holy See over the past forty years or so been followed with understanding and generosity ?

On a lower level we find God's guidance in the works of theologians and spiritual writers. They must of course be judged in the light of their faithfulness to Revelation and to the Church's authoritative teaching. But, granted that faithfulness, they can be of considerable help by bringing dogma more within our grasp and by applying moral principles to the problems of the type of life we lead. The point does not need elaboration. What does perhaps need to be said is that it is an error to seek God's guidance in such works to the exclusion of the Church's teaching. It is true that they incorporate her teaching. But there is always a time-lag between the voice of the Church and the pen of the writer. More important still, even a good spiritual writer will fail to awaken faith as does, for example, an encyclical. On the one hand we find a writer whose views may be accepted because they are sound common sense, or because of the literary charm of the form he gives them: on the other, the Vicar of Christ, speaking in the exercise of an authority given him by God. It is more important to be up-to-date in regard to pontifical directives than in regard to spiritual literature. The ideal is to keep abreast of both: but to do that with due thought for their hierarchy of values.

*   *   *   *

Joy in the christian life depends so much on submission to God's guidance that it may be well at this point to refer to a possible source of error. It is commonly said that God leads us by His grace. If the word "grace" is taken in its widest possible connotation the statement is open to no misunderstanding. For all God's guidance, whether from within our souls or from outside us, is a favour He grants us in love, and that is what "grace" in its widest connotation means. Unfortunately however, there is a tendency to take the word in the narrower sense of actual grace in the mind and will. In consequence God's guidance of us is reduced to the lights He grants to the mind and the inclinations He impresses on the will. Corresponding to this, submission to His guidance is reduced to a careful attention to interior lights and urges. Such a concept of God's guidance is nothing but a new form of the old errors of illuminism, enthusiasm and private judgment. While it is perfectly true, and consoling to remember, that Gods acts within us, it is necessary to bear in mind that His interior guidance is normally conditioned by His exterior guidance through the Church. Thus, He enlightens the mind to accept what the Church teaches; He moves the will to execute what the Church advises and commands. It is not necessary to repeat here what has been said already about the different ways in which the Church teaches and directs us. It is abundantly clear that in one way or another the Church has something to say in every problem of faith or conduct. God's interior guidance is therefore, not restricted by the fact that it works within the framework of the Church. Rather is the framework of the Church's action so comprehensive that it allows for the differing needs of individuals, ages and conditions. That is part of the mystery of the Church instituted by Jesus as the unique and all-sufficient general means of salvation to mankind.

The catholic tendency is therefore to look outside oneself for the pattern of God's guidance. Beyond the fact that this means turning to the Church and to every source (theologians, spiritual writers, preachers and so on) in which her teaching may be found, it involves two other points which deserve attention.

The first is that God's guidance, though so closely connected with the Church, makes full allowance for the personal factor. Wishing to lead a more active christian life, a person joins a catholic action organization. After some time in it he finds that it makes no appeal to him. More than that, it makes him irritable and slightly cynical. What is he to do. Quite clearly to leave the organization and, perhaps, look for another more congenial one; not, however, precisely on the grounds that it conflicted with his inner lights and urges, but on the objective grounds that a voluntary work ought to be of the kind that one can give oneself to with conviction, and that, in any case, a voluntary work which seems to be an occasion of sin is better dropped or replaced by something else. In other words, the problem is solved by weighing up the personal factor in accordance with the teaching of moral and ascetical theology which is one of the voices by which the Church speaks.

The second point is that God's guidance is found more clearly indicated in the external setting of one's life than in interior attractions. If we open our eyes to the little world that surrounds us we shall at once see a hundred things we could and perhaps ought do. Shutting our eyes and waiting for an interior light may merely result in wanting to do something that may never be possible for us or useful for anyone else. Even in matters of vocation and the call to greater perfection the indications suggested by external circumstances may be decisive. An active missionary in an understaffed mission feels drawn to the contemplative life. Are not the souls around him who will be left shepherdless if he retires to a monastery a clearer indication of where God is leading him than his interior feeling? Perhaps the feeling, if it is good at all, is there just to make him think a little more seriously of the interior life, not to draw him from the immediate service of souls. A father of a young family may feel drawn to spending long hours in prayer. If he follows that inclination, his family will suffer in various ways. Clearly his first duty is to them. He may try to fit more prayer into his life—and likely enough it will be possible to do so—but not so much as to lead to neglect of his children. Our christianity is a living thing not precisely because it is the expression of consciously felt inner urges but because personal knowledge and personal love go into it. Where there is knowledge of the way one follows and love of it, there is a truly personal and fully accepted life. By the knowledge of faith and the love of charity we can make our acceptance of God's guidance personal and fully vital.

    *   *   *   *

In order that God's Providence be a source of joy and peace it is therefore necessary that it be accepted in love: or we might speak rather of the need for trust, for repose in God and in the belief that He loves us and wills our good. The more fully we commit ourselves to God's guidance the deeper our peace. We must become little children in our acceptance of God's will: accepting it without question and trusting implicitly that there is love in it. ". . . whosoever shall not receive the kingdom of God as a little child shall not enter into it".[5] Childhood and the peace of childhood cannot, however, be ours if we are men, jealous of our self-will and our self-determination. To find our lives we must lose them: we must renounce the desire to be masters of our fate and put ourselves quite simply and trustingly in God's hands. If we try to save our lives, that is, to keep them entirely ours and fully under our own exclusive control, we lose them.

Speaking of the place of obedience in the religious life, St. Thomas has much to say which can easily be applied to the wider question of childhood in the christian life. The religious life, he tells us, is a *disciplina,* that is a process of education, training or soul-formation. But education presupposes an educator and acceptance of his role by those committed to him. Hence the need of obedience in the religious life, for by it the religious accepts the guidance of his superiors in what concerns his special way of life.[6]

---

[5] Mk. 10, 15.
[6] IIa IIae, Q 186, a5.

In God's plan the world is a school of holiness: a place where holiness is learned and lived. God Himself is our teacher. His teaching is manifold, coming to us through the various channels we have mentioned in this chapter. We learn our lesson of holiness only if we really go to school to God. And that is where becoming a little child is so important. One learns only if there is docility of mind. And when it is life that is being taught, docility of will is needed also. The basic mistake in life would be to accept and live it on one's own terms. One can't go profitably to school that way: neither can one live fruitfully that way. Just the same thing is needed in both cases: the docility which is inborn in a child, for the child feels as well as knows that it is a learner. More than that, the child find joy in being a learner. It finds assurance in trusting itself to its teacher. And this assurance is all the greater if the teacher is loved as well as trusted. When God invites us to be as little children, He does not, therefore, ask of us a mere form of renunciation. He invites us to joy as well: not a joy based on the make-believe of pretending we are children, but a joy based on acceptance of the fact that in the business of life we really are children and He is our Father and our loving teacher.

Ultimately God never asks us to abdicate anything of the dignity of personal responsibility in life. What He asks us is to accept fully life as it truly is. He wants us to put the whole of our minds and the whole of our wills into life, to live as fully responsible beings endowed with the gift of personality. We show our sense of responsibility by recognizing that in the spiritual order we are children. The joy that follows therefrom is no petty reward of immature escapism. It is but the logical consequence of being mature enough to know our immaturity, of being realist enough to commit ourselves to Him in Whom is life.

9

CHARITY AND JOY

Some few years ago I brought the Last Sacraments to a leper. He lived in a very backward place where there were no facilities for treating his disease. To-day one can with difficulty find a like place, such has been the progress in providing medical care for the outcast. He had been given a hut apart on the outskirts of his village, so small that there was little more than room to lie down within it. Kind friends brought him his meals and looked after his principal needs. But for most of the day and all the night he was alone, slowly wasting away. When I visited him he had but a short time to live. Worn out and listless he awaited death, lacking almost all the comforts with which we love to surround the dying. He received the Sacraments with quiet peaceful devotion, his face calm but expressionless. Before leaving I said a few words to him about God and heaven. At once his face lit up. He had forgotten the misery of his long years of suffering. The love of God and the desire of God welled up to the surface of his soul and invested even his broken body with serene dignity. There in that leper's hut were peace and joy called down on earth by the love of a child for his Father.

The same peace and joy can be found in any contemplative monastery or in any christian home where God is loved. It is found also wherever our neighbour is loved and served, for with one and the same love we love God Himself and our neighbour for His sake. One cannot visit a hospital or orphanage or home for the aged or any similar institution conducted by religious without noting the joy with which they devote themselves to their life of service. The same is true of christian layfolk who are engaged in any charitable work. Joy is characteristic of the christian social worker, the christian lay apostle, the christian who in any capacity whatever offers his life for the good of others. Those who leave all for Jesus' sake and to continue His saving work on earth, find that in His goodness He gives them back a hundredfold what they have renounced. Charity works a double blessing: it blesses him who is charitable and him to whom he is charitable. We find our lives by losing them in the service of God and our neighbour. We lose them if we aim at exploiting them selfishly.

Thus, though all the virtues yield joy, charity does so in a pre-eminent manner. Love causes joy and communicates joy to all it touches. If we love, we find joy in what we do in love. Love transforms duties. It makes burdens light. It sweetens what is distasteful and gives charm to what is wearisome.

Charity is given to us with the grace of God. Anyone who is not in the state of mortal sin has it within him to love God and his neighbour and to rejoice in that love. Why then do we love so little and experience so little of love's fruits? The reason is that our love is hampered both in its exercise and in its growth. Charity is the queen of the virtues. It bears fruit fully in us only if we allow it really to reign. We must remove what is opposed to it: we must strive unceasingly to grow in it. To do this is to measure up to our vocation as christians. For love is the summary of all that God asks of us. Every attempt we make to become more to God's heart is an attempt to grow in love.

Growth in charity being, then, in effect, growth in the whole spiritual life, it is neither necessary nor possible to treat of it adequately here. Instead we may consider just one point: how is it that charity so diffuses joy through life? What is there in charity which gives it the power to transform service into devotedness?

The old scholastic definition tells us that to love is to wish well to another. Let us adapt it slightly and say that to love is to be able to wish well to another. For we are concerned here with the power that love gives rather than with its manner of acting. Charity is poured into our souls by God. It is within us awaiting use. It is not a skill to be acquired— though its increases with use. It is a skill given to us by God and of so wonderful a kind that only with difficulty do we understand how it has transformed us.

The tendency of fallen nature is to use the will for oneself. We regard it as the faculty whose special work is to see that we get what we want. Once the heart is set on a thing, the will tries to procure it. And all the faculties of man that are under the control of his will, as well as everything outside him that he can bend to obedience to his will, is enlisted for that purpose under the will's leadership. The fallen will is preoccupied with what is good for self. That is its passion. In attaining that good it experiences its warped joy. One of the effects of the grace of God is to undo the baneful effects which original sin has had on the will. By the virtue of charity we are empowered to turn outside ourselves, in supernatural and unselfish love, to others—to God and to our neighbour. Charity will not, of course, act without our co-operation: we must do a real violence to our self-centredness and must deliberately accept the new orientation which charity gives to our wills. But the really big thing to note is not that we have to do our share: it is that grace has given us a possibility of doing something of which, of ourselves, we are utterly incapable. It had added a new dimension to life, a dimension where we escape from the confinement of self-love and meet God and souls. In that encounter is joy, and the highest joy this world can give.

That, then, is the really wonderful thing about charity: that it enables us to put God and souls where fallen nature puts self. The old man finds his will absorbed by self and finds his pleasure in using it for self: the new man of grace finds that his will can be absorbed in God and souls and that he can find joy in loving and serving them. Charity is like a new centre of gravity—more precisely, it is like a new magnetic pole drawing the will and giving the will rest. The christian can rejoice in serving others in a higher and more satisfying way than the non-christian rejoices in caring for himself. Still more can the christian rejoice in God. This is but an aspect of the rebirth which our admission to the faith implies: "Unless a man be born again of water and the Holy Ghost, he cannot enter into the kingdom of God".[1] Christianity is no mere veneer which leaves the depths of the soul and its most cherished urges untouched. It is a radical transformation: so radical that we can speak, in a sense, of a complete emptying of the christian's being: not an emptying which results in loss, but one which makes possible the great gain of entry to God and to souls made in His image and likeness.

* * * *

St. Thomas Aquinas' treatment of *amor* (love) and *caritas* (charity) in the Summa Theologica is among the most rewarding in his whole synthesis of christian morality. The point we have made just now concerning what might be called the outwardness of charity, is to be found in his article on the relation between love and ecstasy.[2] Ecstasy is a going out of oneself, a being outside oneself. Love effects this by moving the lover to will good to the loved one, and procure good for him, as it were caring for him and providing for him for his own sake. St. Thomas is not, of course, speaking here of ecstasy in the popular sense of the term, where the soul becomes so absorbed in God as to lose or almost lose consciousness of self.[3] But the popular sense of the term is close enough to his technical sense to throw some light on it. The loss of self-consciousness occasioned by the soul's outward movement to God is a forceful reminder of the self-forgetfulness and the godwardness that is in every act of charity. We

[1] Jo. 3, 5.
[2] Ia IIae, Q 28, a 3.
[3] He treats of this elsewhere as rapture: IIa IIae, Q 175.

are all ecstatics in St. Thomas' sense of the word, and the more ecstatic the more christian.

Among the many other pages which St. Thomas devoted to love and charity, I should like to draw attention to those in the IIa IIae, Q28, where he treats of gaudium or joy. Joy he tells us, is in a special way the fruit of charity and most particularly of charity as directed towards God. A person rejoices both when his friend is with him and when his friend has all that is needed for his own happiness. The first of these joys is reserved in its highest form for eternity. Then only will God be fully present to us and we to Him. Here on earth we have it only imperfectly, just as our possession of God by grace is imperfect. The second of these joys is also found in its highest in heaven; there only do we see how wonderfully perfect God is, how infinitely happy. On earth it is, however, possible to us in some small but real measure. For faith tells us that God is infinitely perfect, that in Him is fulness of life, that He is the Supreme Lord and Majesty in Whose presence all things are as nothing. Hence, we can rejoice even now in God's Perfection. And it is good for us to do so. In His unchanging Perfection we have the one fixed point in a changing universe . . . Whatever else we rejoice in grows and decays, is and ceases to be. God alone remains forever, and forever the same. This aspect of charity is proposed to us in many liturgical and traditional prayers, nowhere, perhaps, more strikingly than in the "Gloria in Excelsis Deo . . .": "We praise Thee, we bless Thee, we adore Thee, we glorify Thee. We give Thee thanks for Thy great glory. . ." Right down through the prayer we exult in God being all that He is, and nowhere is that more clear than in the last phrase quoted: "We give Thee thanks for Thy great glory." To thank God that He is so glorious: what a wonderful act of love that is, what a wonderful way to rejoice in Him ! It is as if we felt that God's advantage is our advantage, His greatness as near to our hearts as our own. It is in fact more than that. To love God in an ordered way is to put Him immeasurably before self. It is, therefore, to hold His advantage and His greatness as more our concern than what affects us in a purely personal way. Only by meditating on the implications of prayers such as the *Gloria* can we come to a realization of what charity does within us. Pray that it produce its full effect. Pray that it put God where sin would put self. Pray that it make Him the heart of your heart and the centre of every desire. Then will you find that he who abides in charity abides in God, and the God of all peace and consolation abides in him.

Love of God prompts us also to work for His glory, both by ourselves keeping His commandments and by helping others to do the same. Work done thus for God in charity is a source of joy, for charity makes God dearer to us— immeasurably dearer than our own selves. Our whole heart and soul and strength and mind are not enough to spend for God if we truly love Him. This is a point with which we are all familiar. For that reason it is not necessary to develop it here. Instead we may pass on at once to the matter of joy in charity towards our neighbour.

* * * *

Since it is by the same love that we love God and our neighbour, we find joy in the love of our neighbour also. There are two ways in which this happens. The first is when our love rests with satisfaction in the spiritual graces with which our neighbour is endowed. The second is when our love prompts us to procure for him the graces and other benefits of which he stands in need.

The first way of loving our neighbour is analogous to that outlined above as one of the ways of loving God. It is most advantageous to remember that it is also a way of loving our neighbour. It is a way which we are strongly tempted, when we practise it at all, to confine to our relations with canonized saints. One of the ways in which we love them is, in fact, to rejoice that they are in glory, and that they are honoured on earth by men. But even in regard to the saints it is a way not often adverted to, and in regard to our as yet uncanonized fellow-mortals it is still more neglected. Charity prompts us to be glad that others are close friends of God, that they serve Him with generosity, that their work for Him is crowned with success. It leads us to make joyfully the discovery that all are not so niggardly with God as we are, to be happy that He is served well by them and that they have drawn near to Him. Under this respect charity is at the opposite pole to envy and its train of allied vices. In the eyes of the envious man his neighbour's virtue and success are causes for dissatisfaction. He looks neither at the glory they give to God nor at the advantage they are to his neighbour who is God's child. His whole concern is how they make self appear in self's estimation. And with such a bias, he naturally enough finds that they show self up in an unfavourable light. Charity understands the precept of St. Paul: "Rejoice with them that rejoice; weep with them that weep".[4] Another's gain is reckoned by charity as one's own; another's loss is suffered as something personal; "Charity envieth not . . . seeketh not her own".[5]

The second way of loving our neighbour, and the one which we are called upon most frequently to practise, is to serve him; that is, to help him to acquire the spiritual and material good of which he has need. Just because charity enables us to act towards our neighbour as if he were our own self, service of our neighbour can be joyous: it is as if we were acting in a way that contributed to our personal advantage. That is one of the things implied in loving one's neighbour as oneself. For this does not mean merely to do for him the same kind of things that we do for self: it implies that we do them for him with the same kind of relish that we find in doing them for self. This explains the joy in life of the great saints of charity and of all those lesser souls who follow in their footsteps.

However, because of the innate pettiness which provokes

[4] Rom. 12, 15.
[5] I Cor. 13, 4-5.

us to envy and because also of the attitude of opposition or indifference which our neighbour may adopt towards us, the exercise of fraternal charity, often meets with obstacles which makes it anything but joyous. We may, for example, literally have to force ourselves to act in a christian way towards another whom we dislike, and our natural repugnance to being charitable to him will prevent the joy of charity from being perceived. The same thing happens when we practise charity in regard to one who causes us suffering. The suffering being more clearly registered in our consciousness than the joy of charity, we feel it hard to keep on loving and helping in spite of so much ingratitude. It is therefore evident that charity towards our neighbour is not always experienced as a joyous act. But that is not to be wondered at. It is just one of the ways in which the imperfection of the beatitude of earth makes itself felt. Only in heaven will our joy be full. On earth there is always some admixture of pain, some diminution of joy: but never such as of necessity to take away our peace of soul. Peace, at least, we can always experience in our practice of charity. When we find that even our peace is disturbed, we must seek the explanation in ourselves rather than in others. Opposition and ingratitude may pain us: they cannot take away our peace of soul. Only our own evil dispositions, our envy, our ill-concealed hatred, our desire for revenge and all our other forms of self-centredness, are capable of reducing the effort to be charitable to embittered failure. Others cannot poison our relations with them: we alone can do that. And, in that sense, the joy and peace of love of our neighbour depend on us and on no one else. Others may to some extent be responsible for the pain that their actions cause us: we alone are responsible if they cause us loss of peace.

*   *   *   *

In the same twenty-eighth question of the *Secunda Secundae* of St. Thomas to which reference has been made above, we find a most interesting reference to the fact that charity, as well as causing joy, can in certain circumstances cause a certain type of pain. Thus, whereas charity rejoices in God's Infinite Perfection, it finds reason for grief in the fact that He is so much offended by sin and so little glorified by men. And the greater the charity the greater the grief so caused. Something similar can be said of charity in regard to our neighbour. The more truly we love souls the more we suffer at the thought of the danger in which sin and vice places them. Here we have a charity that weeps with them that weep: weeping with God as He would weep were He a man and capable of suffering; weeping with sinners as they would weep if they were saints and knew the full enormity of sin.

This grief, which is, as it were, the very child of charity, is no obstacle to peace of soul. Its immediate effect is to move us to work in love and patience that God's rights be more fully admitted and that men accept His law. It has nothing in common with the fretful grief which wounded self-love causes. The latter grief produces turmoil in the soul. It is essentially disordered and is the enemy of peace, which is the tranquillity of order. Grief that God's rights are denied or that a soul is in danger is an ordered grief. It is caused by a disorder outside the soul: in itself, however, it is the soul's ordered reaction to a disordered situation. There is something in it of the patience and long-suffering of God Who without diminution of peace can contemplate sin in the world and work for its destruction. This peace is vitally necessary for the active apostle whose ministry brings him into close contact with sin and opposition to God's plan for the world's salvation. Without it his efforts may degenerate into querulous impatience with those whom he is called to treat with a compassionate and understanding love. It is necessary for the contemplative soul also. For however great the pain felt by the contemplative at the insults offered to God, Jesus' cry " Father forgive them, for they know not what they do " may never be forgotten. Evil is overcome by good. Evil may never drive mercy and forgiveness from our souls. " Charity hopeth all things, endureth all things "[6] It achieves its purpose in patience and not otherwise.

*　　　　*　　　　*　　　　*

Thus far we have considered joy as the fruit of charity. It may be considered under another aspect also, as a condition of soul which favours growth in charity. This second aspect is no less important than the first for the practice of the christian life. In fact, it may with truth be said that one of the great obstacles to the growth of a vigorous charity is precisely lack of joy or enthusiasm.

No one ever throws himself fully into anything about which he is not in some degree at least enthusiastic. If we understand enthusiasm in a spiritual sense, and not as a mere emotional condition, this is true of the christian life no less than of anything else. St. Francis de Sales develops this idea in a simple but amazingly profound way in his "Introduction to the Devout Life". His general theme is that to love God fully we need devotion. Without devotion we may love Him in a certain measure and at certain times. With devotion we love Him with our whole heart and soul and at all times. Following up this general principle, he reduces the whole of the practices of the spiritual life to the effort to acquire and grow in devotion.

For a full and inspiring treatment of this idea one can do no better than to turn to St. Francis de Sales. I shall confine myself here to the points which have a specially close connection with our main thesis.

Devotion arises almost naturally in the soul which regards the spiritual life as essentially a joyous one. Devotion is, in fact, what we more commonly term "devotedness": a truly devout person is a devoted one. Devotion is devotedness to God and to our neighbour, devotedness to their interests, devotedness to their service. While it is theoretically possible to be faithful to God and to our neighbour without experiencing any great enthusiasm for the order of relations

---

[6] I Cor. 13, 7.

in which we are placed in their regard, devotedness to them without enthusiasm is a contradiction in terms. Hence the importance of joy in the spiritual life: for joy in the spiritual life is a form of enthusiasm about it. I am not speaking here, of course, of the emotional joy and enthusiasm of the beginner whom God is aiding with the grace of consolation. I mean a joy and enthusiasm of the spirit, joy and enthusiasm of the will and grace. It is an enthusiasm which means being captured by love and finding all one's peace and joy in living by love. It is an enthusiasm which survives pain, which is compatible with pain. As St. Augustine might have put it, it is a love which has become a weight pressing the soul onwards, a kind of gravitational force drawing it to God. Joy is of the very texture of this enthusiasm—joy and peace. Love which works in a climate of joy and peace is devotion.

Hence the importance of joy or peace of soul in the spiritual life. Without it love cannot reach its full stature. All that has been said about growth in joy can be applied to growth in love and devotion. There is just one point I should like to refer explicitly to, namely, that we ought to pray for the grace of devotion. Devotion is worth praying for. It is a grace God wants to give if only we are disposed to receive it. And as a means of obtaining devotion, let us pray for more joy in life: let us pray that christian living, in its widest and richest sense, may become a passion with us, an all-absorbing interest.

I have mentioned that devotion is not to be confused with spiritual consolations or with any form of joy which the senses may experience in loving God. This does not mean that consolations—to confine ourselves to the one term—are of negligible importance. We are spiritually weak. Normally we need consolations at the beginning of our spiritual lives. And unless we are given a grace of exceptional generosity, they will be useful to us throughout the course of our lives: for so long do we remain weak.

Hence, consolations serve a useful if subsidiary purpose in strengthening our inner devotion. We may be devoted to God, but not devoted enough to give ourselves fully to Him in love without the added stimulus of the joy of consolation. Hence, there is no reason why we should not pray for consolation, if God sees fit to answer our prayer. In fact, there is every reason to pray for it, in a spirit of deep humility, if we find that we are cold in regard to God and in consequence ungenerous with Him. He may not, of course, answer our prayer directly. He may grant us an increase of inner devotion without any corresponding increase of consolation. How He will answer is His secret. What is of importance for us is to realize that we are weak enough to need consolation, leaving it to Him to decide how He will come to the relief of our weakness.

*   *   *   *

Joy is no less important as a condition for the generous practice of love of our neighbour. If we are in any degree discontented with the spiritual life, with our religious or priestly vocation, the discontent will almost certainly manifest itself in impatience with or harshness towards others. A man cannot spend himself in the service of others who is only half-hearted in his own acceptance of life. It is true, of course, that many a disillusioned man has found a new interest in life through throwing himself into a work of charity or service; for charity, as we have seen already, is a source of joy. The point we are making here is somewhat different: it is that a person whose habitual attitude to life is joyless will not find it easy to be charitable to others while still remaining within the old joyless framework. A joyless nurse will hardly be a devoted one. Neither will a joyless teacher, or a joyless religious, or a joyless priest. From time to time we have all met dissatisfied people who made life difficult for those around them. They were lacking in sympathy and understanding: only rarely did they lend a helping hand. They were critical of others, impatient with their faults, distrustful of change, intolerant of forms of piety which were not their own. The root cause of their lack of charity was their joyless concept of life. Perhaps they were conscientious in the performance of their personal obligations and duties. Perhaps they were models of exterior observance. But there was something about them which made them a standing reproach: dissatisfied with life as they found it, they could hardly be expected to be satisfied with it as found in others.

We have already seen how important this point may be in the time of suffering. Suffering may embitter a person, turning him in upon himself. The cases we have mentioned just now indicate the same lesson, though with a difference. For they are not cases of suffering so much as cases of mere joylessness. It also can embitter and turn a person in upon himself. The reason is simple: it is that life as God gave it and as man wants to live it is not intended to be joyless. God made us for joy: we for our part want it intensely. If we fail to find it, and, most particularly, if we come to the false position that life is a joyless experience, the heart is taken out of our efforts and generosity becomes virtually impossible.

" He who soweth sparingly shall also reap sparingly; and he who soweth in blessings shall also reap in blessings. Every one as he hath determined in his heart, not with sadness or of necessity; for God loveth a cheerful giver"[7]. St. Paul is speaking here of the collections which were made for the poor of the early Church and is recommending the Corinthians to give gladly and generously. But, as is so commonly the case with him, his thought overflows the immediate context and he touches on wide general principles. There ought to be in our relations with God and man a certain spaciousness. Living life to the full does not mean doling out a minimum of what we owe to God and man.

---

[7]II Cor. 9, 6-7.

If we think and act on such parsimonious lines we ourselves are the first to suffer: for if we sow sparingly we shall reap sparingly too in life's harvest. In all that we do there ought to be an element of generosity. We have made up in our heart that true life is to be found in God and in our neighbour. It was not an admission wrung grudgingly from us, but one in the nature of an exhilarating discovery. And in joy—the joy of the man who found the hidden, unrecognized treasure, and gave all he had to procure it—we throw ourselves unreservedly into life. That means giving—giving to God and giving to men. But we give in joy; and because of the joy there is all the more of ourselves in the giving. Nor is it only giving. If we give to God or to the least of His children in His name, we receive from Him a hundredfold. God loves the cheerful giver and shows His love by Himself giving grace.

It is unfortunate that so many people's experience of the faith in action has been through contacts with more or less soured christians engaged in one form or another of the active life. Nothing can give a falser notion of christianity than a cheerlessness which has been accepted as a philosophy of life. Christianity is not the door to mere pleasure. Of necessity the Cross goes with it. But through and through it is joyous, and one of the aims of the christian—priest or religious or layman—engaged in the active apostolate ought to be to embody his own inner peace and contentment in his relations with those he works for. Thank God, the world is full of christians who do that. Without their even speaking a word, their lives are a sufficient lesson in the meaning and attractiveness of christianity. God loves them for their cheerfulness, often enough wrung from the bitterness of suffering. And in their cheerfulness He sees the promise, planted by Him within them, of more than common holiness.

Those of us who are engaged in the active life ought then to pray for joy in the service of our neighbour. To serve

our neighbour at all is to that extent to love him. To serve
him in joy is more. It is to love him with devotion.

*   *   *   *

Charity reaches its climax in heaven. So does our joy.
It is a sublimely fitting thing that beatific joy should reside
in the will. For the will is the faculty which, more than
any other, has borne the labour and the heat of life's short
day. Strengthened particularly by hope and charity, the
will has kept up its tendency towards God. On it devolved
the labour of marshalling all our other powers in His love
and service. It was the will, too, strengthened by grace,
which kept us at the arduous task of working for our
neighbour's salvation. During our life on earth the intellect
has the relatively easy task of seeing what is to be done,
what is worth-while doing, and how to set about it. The
will's is the more difficult one of conquering sluggishness,
self-centredness, fear, love of pleasure and all the other
tendencies and weakness which keep us from following
the path the mind sees traced clearly before it. The will,
therefore, which is on earth the principle of our tending
towards God, has reserved for it in heaven the reward of
being the faculty which rests in Him. Striving, straining,
tending cease in eternity. There God is held in vision, never
to be lost, never to be sought for. And the will enters into
its rest, a rest of love, a rest of beatific joy. The joy of
heaven is one which springs from love that has found Him
Whom it loves: it is charity in its full flowering, charity
revealing to the soul those full potentialities which on earth
could never be completely realized.

Though charity cannot unfold itself fully while we still
remain clothed in mortal flesh, it ought to be a source of
joy and encouragement to us, that the same charity that
we shall relish in heaven is ours even now. Faith and hope,
glorious virtues though they are, are for this life only: with
God seen in vision and possessed in face to face embrace
they will have lost their purpose and function. Charity will

endure. Absent or present to us, God is always to be loved. True, our love in heaven will be something far more perfect than our love of Him on earth. But it will be, in its essence, the same love, differing only in the perfection of its act. Then it will be a love such as we can barely conceive of now: a love that clings to God as the All, as nearer to us—unspeakably nearer—than we are to our own selves. Clinging so to Him, accepting Him as the heart and centre of our being, we shall find that in Him we have received all that is good, even a share in the gladness of his own beatific joy.

10

MARY, CAUSE OF OUR JOY

GOD has given to Mary, Mother of the Redeemer and of the Redeemed, a place of such importance in the spiritual life that no aspect of it can be adequately understood without reference to her. Joy is no exception to this rule. To confirm the fact that Mary is intimately connected with our joy, we may appeal to the invocation so widely used with ecclesiastical approval throughout the Church: Cause of our joy, pray for us. In this, the last chapter of the book, it is proposed to examine the implications of so addressing her.

Every prerogative, every spiritual endowment of Mary comes to her through Jesus. It is through Jesus that she is cause of our joy. And this, first of all, because she gave us Jesus, in Whom we have access to God, the Fount of all joy.

Mary gave us Jesus. She was really and truly consulted by God about the Incarnation. God asked her consent to be the Mother of the Redeemer. By her fiat she opened the way to Jesus' entry to the world. Hence she is cause of our joy as being the one who agreed to God's proposal that He should be born through Whom we have joy. Far be it from us to think that this is but a distant connection with joy. Mary did not consent to something the meaning of which was hidden from her. True, she did not at the moment of the Incarnation understand God's plans as fully as she would later, with the gradual maturing of

153

her fulness of grace. But she knew at least that she was consenting to something which would be a blessing for mankind, something which would mark the beginning of their liberation from the consequences of sin and their entry into a new intimacy with their Father in Heaven. Thus, even if the word "joy" did not pass through her mind—and it is hard to imagine that she could have failed to see joy in God's proposed coming among men—the idea of joy was in its substance present to her. God's offer, she must have understood, was an offer of joy to all men, and she by accepting it willed that men should have joy. Her fiat therefore caused our joy: the joy we have in Jesus now was implicit in what Mary willed to give us.

Mary's understanding of her role in God's redemptive plan grew with the years. And with that understanding grew her desire to give Jesus more and more to mankind: her desire and the prayer in which she expressed it, was, in fact, already a new giving of Jesus to men, a further realization of what she had begun when she said "yes" to God in Nazareth. She reached a decisive stage in this process on Calvary. There it became crystal clear to her what it meant to give Jesus to men and what it meant to men to have Jesus given to them. The point is brought home to us at one of the stations of the Cross which, even though it may not be historically true, lays bare what took place in the interior of Jesus and Mary. It is the station where we find Jesus and Mary meeting on the way to Calvary. Mary suffered inexpressibly in her human heart at the sight of what Jesus was enduring and at the thought of what He had yet to endure. Jesus too suffered that His mother was not spared the vision of His Passion and death. From both hearts there arose the prayer: Father, if it be possible that this chalice pass from me, from my Son, from my Mother. But it was a prayer enclosed within a still deeper one: Yet not my will but Thine be done. Mary was willing, and her soul was at peace, that Jesus should die for mankind. Meeting Him on the way to Calvary, she signified her consent to His death by following Him to the foot of the Cross where she took her stand in spiritual union with Him. Thinking of us she willed our joy through Jesus' pain and hers. "A woman, when she is in labour, hath sorrow because her hour is come; but when she hath brought forth the child, she remembereth no more the anguish, for joy that a man is brought forth into the world"[1]. Calvary was the hour of bringing forth the Mystical Body, the hour when through Jesus Mary brought forth mankind to the life and joy of grace. Somewhat as St. Paul says of Jesus that, having joy set before Him, He endured the cross (Hebr 12,2) we may say of Mary that she endured it also for the sake of the joy that was to be His and hers and ours. In God's designs Calvary called for that participation of hers, just as her participation was called for at Nazareth more than thirty years before. And through that participation she became in an even fuller sense the cause of our joy.

*   *   *   *

Granted then this fundamental fact that through her union with Jesus Mary was allowed to give us as Co-redemptrix all that christianity holds out to us, we may consider some of the many ways in which we find our joy in her. The first is by turning to her as the model of christian joy.

Let us go back to Nazareth. God's will was made known to Mary through the message of the angel. Her reaction was to accept in love and humility. Zachary had hesitated in similar circumstances and had been punished. Mary embraced God's will as soon as it was clear to her, and in doing so found peace, for His will is our peace. The first lesson Mary teaches us is therefore that joy is found in conformity to the will of God. His purposes may be hidden from us: what He asks may involve many a

---

[1] Jo. 16, 21.

sacrifice. But His thoughts are always thoughts of peace and love, and in His will our souls find rest as Mary's did.

Mary's peace was not a selfish one. Called to be Mother of the Saviour she was called to take mankind to her heart. Thus it is that we find her setting out at once to the home of her cousin Elizabeth, who needed her help and whose yet unborn child would be sanctified at her presence. Mary did not therefore find joy in God to the exclusion of her neighbour. Like us, her joy was to love God and men, to serve God and men. Filled with the Holy Ghost, Elizabeth called her blessed—a word rich in meaning which implied among other things that the favour she enjoyed in God's eyes placed her on an unequalled eminence of serene joy. At Elizabeth's words Mary's tongue gave utterance to the emotions that the events of the previous days had caused to well up in her soul: My spirit hath rejoiced in God my Saviour. Joy was hers as the result of her obedience: joy was hers as the result of her intimacy with the Incarnate Word living in her womb: joy was hers in moving among men as one who brought them Jesus. The hungry had been filled with good things, those who hungered for abundant life. Through Jesus and His Mother they would be so filled to the end of time. Her heart was full of all that God had done to her. She could find no more appropriate way to express her gratitude than to begin to share her fulness with others.

I have mentioned first of all how Mary found joy in serving others, for such is the order in which St. Luke's Gospel narrates the events which surround the Incarnation. Her prayer, the Magnificat, however reminds us that the deep fount of her joy was God: My spirit hath rejoiced in God my Saviour. Mary is a model to those who seek God in prayer and contemplation. She tells us that it is in Him that we find our greatest joy. A young inexperienced girl, living in a backward part of a backward country, unversed in what the great civilizations and cultures could offer, she found complete satisfaction in God. Hers was the short-cut to the goal of happiness all men seek. Saints like Augustine would bewail that they had found happiness late. Sinners have found in their declining years that the happiness they thought they had found had all the while eluded them. She, whom the world would have considered ignorant—knowing little more than God, and knowing that little in relation to Him, was already full of grace and joy. With the birth and the growth of the God-man, her Son, she would continue to find her peace in God. All Jesus' words, all His actions, would be treasured in her heart: held there as of inestimable value, held there to be relished even when not fully understood. For most of her life she comes before us as the contemplative. Not as the contemplative cut away from social intercourse, for she was mother of a family, mistress of a household and helpful friend to her neighbours—but as the contemplative whose cloister is the soul shared with God. We see in her how we active christians of today can joy in God. We pray to her that we may joy in Him as she did.

I have already spoken of suffering in Mary's life. She is our model of peace in suffering. Sorrowing she sought Jesus during the three days' loss. His words to her when she found Him in the temple may well have been her decisive lesson in the mysterious marriage between joy and pain. For, though she did not at once grasp all that His pregnant words expressed—"And they understood not the word that He spoke to them"[2]—she treasured them in her heart, grace slowly distilling from them their deep significance. They prepared her for the long separation of Jesus' public life, and for the separation, more painful still, which took place on Calvary. We may well believe that when Mary first sought Jesus sorrowing, her sorrow though real was not such as to shatter her peace of soul.

---

[2] Lk. 2, 50.

This peace in suffering became even clearer as she advanced in years and grace. We see it in her dignified seclusion when Jesus set out on His active ministry. We see it finally as she stands at the foot of the cross: erect, courageous, peaceful; not broken and vainly repining. Of Mary the Church says: Whose sorrow is like unto my sorrow? We may add: Whose peace in sorrow is like unto my peace? She suffered for God and Man. She suffered freely and with a sublime understanding of suffering's value: *Juxta crucem tecum stare, Et me tibi sociare, In planctu desidero.*[3]

*   *   *   *

Mary is more than our model in joy. We receive joy from her hands. This is but an aspect of the doctrine that she dispenses all graces, in complete dependence on her Divine Son.

In a book which is not a treatise on Mariology one is not expected to go in detail into the question of the manner in which Mary dispenses grace—including the grace of spiritual joy. There are theologians who, for example, hold that her dispensing of graces has in it something of physical and efficient causality. Leaving such technical points aside, and without prejudice to what might be said for or against the view that Mary's causation of grace is physical, it will be sufficient here to recall that on any hypothesis her influence will certainly include an element of impetration: that is to say, one of the ways in which Mary most certainly dispenses grace is by her unceasing petition to the Father through Jesus for the graces we need.[4] This petition of hers, we remember, is more than a wish which may be disregarded. When she asks for grace, it is for a grace over which her union with Jesus on

---

[3]"By the Cross with you to be, Sharing sorrow's company, Mary, is my heart's desire."—from the Stabat Mater.

[4]This does not make the sacraments superfluous or their action uncertain. For Mary asks for grace through Jesus and in accordance with the system He established for its communication to souls.

Calvary has given her certain claims. Moreover, united to God in the beatific vision, she asks not in an arbitrary way, but in union with His infinitely merciful and compassionate will. Her impetration is, therefore, supremely efficacious. She is a true Queen, and by her prayer disposes with Queenly authority of the treasures of the Kingdom of heaven.

She is mother also. And that is, perhaps, the point on which we prefer to linger. For a mother is intensely interested in the joy of her child. A mother is not satisfied that her child have what is good for it: she wants it to be happy in the possession of its good. A mother is quick to notice the uneasiness that may be hidden in the heart of an apparently successful son of hers. She may say nothing: she does not wish to add sorrow to sorrow. But she tries to find out what is wrong and then to fill the void she has discovered. Mary has this mother's interest in our happiness even while we are on earth and strives to secure happiness no less than grace and virtue for us. In this, of course, she is but God's instrument. For God is to us a mother no less than a father: in Him, as in the Fount of all good, is what makes both fatherhood and motherhood what they are. But He uses Mary when He wishes to be motherly towards us. More than that, she is, as it were, the guarantee of His Motherliness. Having introduced her into the heart of His designs for men He could not, without contradicting Himself, cease to treat us in a motherly way.

Mary is then cause of our joy both by procuring joy for us through her prayer and by guaranteeing God's unchangeable will to grant us joy. The Church applies to Mary those words once spoken in praise to Judith: " Thou art the glory of Jerusalem, thou art the joy of Israel."[5] Mary is our glory and our joy. Through her, who suffered that we might be born to grace, we taste the sweetness of being to God as most dear children.

---

[5] Judith, 15, 10

There are other ways also in which Mary is cause of our joy. For example, there is the way by which she confirms our hope.

Hope consists primarily in reliance on the Power of God to provide us with grace in this world and with glory in the world to come. But its actual exercise is influenced by a number of other virtues. For example, a person may lose hope through lack of fortitude. He may lose hope also through lack of love of God, for it is not usual to rely on someone whom we do not love. This connection of hope with other virtues suggests how Mary may influence our hope, even though it is a theological virtue which has God Himself as its motive. Loving and trusting and relying on Mary is a help to loving and trusting and relying on God: not that she is more worthy of love and trust and reliance than God is—the idea is ridiculous—but because being less than Him, nearer to our level and more easily understood by us, we may pass from her to Him: she helps us to rise from reliance on our Mother, who, after all, can do nothing of herself alone, to reliance on our Father to whom she must herself turn. Hence, Mary is closely connected with our joy in hope. With her help we trust more confidently in God for grace and for glory and in that confidence we find peace.

Rather similar to this is Mary's influence on our joy through her connection with God's government of the world. At times we may be tempted to fear that God's dealings with us and with the world are dealings of strict justice. Mary's place in His relations with us reminds us at once how groundless the fear is. Since she is Mediatrix of all graces, God never deals with us independently of her. Her motherly influence can, therefore, be traced in every detail of His government of souls. When He governs us it is as if she governed, she who is our mother. And yet, not quite that. Once more, we recall how immeasurably she falls short of God, how slight is her mother's love for us compared with His Divine love. And so we come back gladly to the thought of God ruling our lives. But, now, all fear is banished. We know Him better through knowing Mary, know more of His tenderness precisely because we have rated hers so highly.

Towards the end of His life on earth Our Blessed Lord encouraged His disciples by telling them that He was about to go to heaven to prepare a place there for them.[6] His Ascension into heaven was to be their anticipated entry there, for He would take possession of it as Head of the Mystical Body and in their names as well as in His own. This idea may be applied also to the glorious Assumption of Our Blessed Lady. Her court in heaven is now set up: she awaits there the immense multitude who have been called to people it. Her court is a home for she is a Queen who is a mother: there she awaits the children whom she loves. Mary throned in heaven is therefore an anticipation of our glory: with her in heaven, we too are in some sense in heaven. In that way also she confirms our hope, changing it from a mere feeling of possibility, which it might become if not fully developed, into something like a partial attainment of the goal. Mary, like Jesus and under Him, has entered heaven to prepare a place there for us. And what does preparation mean in this context if it does not include helping us through life to the place which is to be ours. In Mary's presence in heaven we find assured our eternal happiness and our possibility of attaining to it. That is an assurance to bring joy to our souls.

*   *   *   *

Thus far we have considered Mary as cause of our joy according to the various ways in which she produces its causes within us or sets them in motion. There is another way also in which she is cause of our joy and a most important one: it is that we can and ought to rejoice in her, in her wonderful attributes, in her incomparable glory

---

[6] Jo. 14, 1-2.

in heaven. We have seen already that the christian rejoices in God, not only because of what God does for him but also, and even more, because of what God is in Himself: We thank Thee for thy great glory. In all due proportion this same idea may be transferred to our relations with Mary. The purest form of love of Mary is to allow the will to rest with joy and satisfaction in her wonderful perfection. If loving means to wish what is good to another, the highest love of the most worthy object of love, is to allow the will to rejoice in the good which the loved one possesses. Because men are so needy, both in spiritual and in temporal things, we cannot love them fully without trying in some way—at any rate by our prayers—to procure their good for them. It is true that in His great mercy God allows us to do something like that for Himself: He allows us to work for His glory. The two cases are not, indeed anything like the same, for God does not Himself gain by the glory we procure for Him: the gain is all on our side and on the side of the men whom we help to glorify Him. By working thus for His glory we give expression to our love. But our love of God has another form of expression which is, if anything more divine. It is the love which is happy in God's happiness: love of pure benevolence into which even giving does not enter.

We may love Mary and rejoice in her in a similar way. It is a glorious thing that she is so full of grace, so clothed in queenly dignity, so far removed from the limitations of our earthly existence. Who would dream of feeling aggrieved that Mary is in glory while he still engages in life's struggle? Joy is not a selfish feeling: a mother's joy is in her family more than in herself. We who are children, not mothers, in the spiritual order, are inclined to be self-centred. Grace can overcome that tendency, and turn us outwards to God and Mary, even in our joys. That spiritual outwardness is a thing to be prayed for. It is not that God frowns on the idea of our working for our personal spiritual advantage;

nor that it is possible for a weak human being always to abstract from self, or even to wish to do so. Outwardness is to be prayed for as something to leaven our spiritual life, helping us to the selflessness which is of obligation and introducing us to the joy of heaven where God is all in all.

And this brings us once more to the thought of heaven where we shall be united in God with Mary and the saints. In its essence, the life of heaven is the possession of God. But heaven is more than a detached essence: God has endowed it with features, accidental to it no doubt, which contribute to making it all that the heart of man can desire. One of these features is the company of the saints, among whom Mary holds a pre-eminent place. Mary will, therefore, be a cause of one of the joys of heaven—the joy of being with her, of beholding her, of hearing her speak and of speaking to her: joys, all of them that are nothing in comparison with the joy of being with God, but that are more than sufficient to thrill our human hearts. Even the angels find rapture in Mary's queenly state. Much more will she be the loving admiration of those who are her children. Her grace is mankind's grace. Her triumph is mankind's triumph. To joy in her is in some sense to joy in what we all are through her. That joy, which we taste but imperfectly on earth, we shall experience in all its purity in heaven.

*   *   *   *

It will be appropriate to close this chapter on Our Lady with a brief reference to St. Joseph, her spouse. The appropriateness is there not merely because he is the spouse of Mary and we can hardly recall her name without thinking of his also, but because he is in a very real way linked up with our joy.

We meet St. Joseph but rarely in the Gospels. That makes it all the more significant that on almost every occasion that he crosses its pages we find him burdened with a cause for worry. We meet him faced with the difficult situation of having learned that his espoused wife is with child. We meet him not so very long afterwards with Mary at Bethlehem, where they had gone to give in their names to the census returning-officers; there is no room for them in the inn and Joseph looks vainly for a friendly roof under which Mary may bring her First-born into the world. After that there is the visit of the Wise Men, followed almost at once by the threat to the life of the Child and Joseph's hasty preparations for the flight into Egypt. The trials of life there—and in no matter what circumstances, the life of a refugee family is bound to be a difficult one for its head—are followed by a new anxiety about where to return to in the Holy Land: Bethlehem might not be safe even yet. Within the Temple, on different occasions, Joseph had care brought home to him: once when Simeon prophesied the sorrows that would mark the lives of Jesus and Mary, and a second time when for three whole days Jesus was lost and Mary and Joseph sought Him sorrowing, only to find Him safe and hear from His lips the enigmatic words: How is it that you sought me? Did you not know that I must be about my Father's business?[7] As I have mentioned already, this is an impressive series of pictures of Joseph burdened with care and responsibility, making up very nearly the full total of what the Holy Ghost has told us about him.

Let us pass now from the pages of Gospel history to the sure but less easy-to-read pages of the christian sense of the faithful, and ask: what kind of a man must St. Joseph have been? Was he habitually worried and gloomy, or was he peaceful and joyous in a quiet way? There is no doubt about the answer we shall receive. Were it for no other reason than that he is a great saint we cannot conceive of St. Joseph as having being anything but peaceful and contented in his life. Mary and Jesus could not have been committed to the care of a troubled and dissatisfied

---

[7]Lk. 2, 49.

protector. St. Joseph knew his weakness. He knew how unequal he was of himself to the fulfilment of the role God allotted him. Time and again in the course of his life that was brought home to him. But throughout it all he remained serene. "He shall say to the Lord: Thou art my protector and my refuge: my God, in him will I trust."[8]

It is true that among the few things mentioned about St. Joseph are included the times when an angel came from God to counsel him. We, for our part cannot count on that special assistance. But those were only some of the times when Joseph had need of help and counsel. For the rest he relied on God and was strengthened by Jesus and Mary. Nor did the angel come to relieve him of all anguish, but rather to tell him what he must do: courage and trust were always needed to carry out the angel's instructions. We can, therefore, pray with special confidence to St. Joseph for the grace of peace and joy in life. He has been tried as we are. He had not Mary's fulness of grace to support him, but only a great, though limited measure of the graces we ourselves receive. It is always a help to be able to turn to someone who has gone through the same kind of trials we are enduring and who felt their pain as we do. And it is a wonderful source of encouragement to know that he who was weak is now among the greatest and most powerful saints in heaven—in all probability second only to Our Lady.

If we examine God's plan for man's redemption we find in it, among other things, the deliberate will to manifest both His understanding of the frailty of human nature and the power of His grace to be made perfect in man's infirmity. Thus, we find God taking true human flesh in the Incarnation, living in the weakness of human flesh and yet raising that flesh to the dignity of union with the Divine Nature: One tempted in all things as we are,

---

[8]Ps. 90, 2.

without sin.[9] We find that the Incarnate Word had a human mother, one of our race, but who was so transformed by grace as to be His worthy associate in the work of redemption. And then, as if He felt that there was still something to be made clear, God introduced St. Joseph into the Holy Family, weak as men are, holy as men can be, but not uniquely privileged in grace as Mary was. St. Joseph's appeal lies precisely in this: that in him we see a human nature tainted with original sin but so transformed by grace as to fulfil worthily the sublime duties of husband of the Mother of God and foster-father of God made man. In him we have the Incarnation's clearest example of human frailty renewed and elevated by grace.

Do not let us hesitate to admit how close we are called to resemble St. Joseph. Our lives must be lived with Jesus and Mary, as his was. They are hidden from us by the veils of faith, but Their presence by grace is real. Christ is born anew in each one of us by grace: we are called to foster the life of the new man within our souls. Mary mothers the life of grace within us: it is our duty to co-operate with her. Our personal relations with Jesus and Mary are like those of St. Joseph also, for Jesus was his Redeemer and his Head as well as his foster-child: Mary was for him, as for us, Mother of the Redeemer and His partner in the work of Redemption. Thus, though there was something in Joseph's position as true spouse of Mary and true foster-father of the child Jesus which has no strict parallel in our case, there was much indeed in his life which may be found in ours also. May we not say that he is both the reality and the symbol of the ordinary christian brought by grace into family intimacy with God and with the Mother of God?

*   *   *   *

Christian piety looks to St. Joseph as the patron of a happy death. His last hours, we believe, were comforted

---

[9]Hebr. 4, 15.

by the strengthening and consoling presence of Jesus and Mary. It is in no way far-fetched to look on him also as an appropriate patron of a happy life. For life and death are all of a piece: death is the entry to that eternal life for which mortal life has been a preparation. Joseph's life was made happy by the same thing that made his death happy: the strengthening and consoling presence of Jesus and Mary. And it is good to recall that he was aware and appreciative of their presence even more by faith than by vision. What was human in them he saw: only by faith did he know their power in the order of grace. May we, like him, find our peace and joy of earth in Jesus and Mary. Like him may we be united with Jesus and Mary in the ineffable joy of eternity.